W9-BXN-501

"LET'S FIGHT THE FILTH WITH FORKS AND FLOWERS!"

ON GUERRILLA GARDENING

A HANDBOOK FOR GARDENING WITHOUT BOUNDARIES

RICHARD REYNOLDS
GUERRILLAGARDENING.ORG

BLOOMSBURY

To my mischievous Mother 008

PART ONE: THE MOVEMENT

PART TWO: THE MANUAL

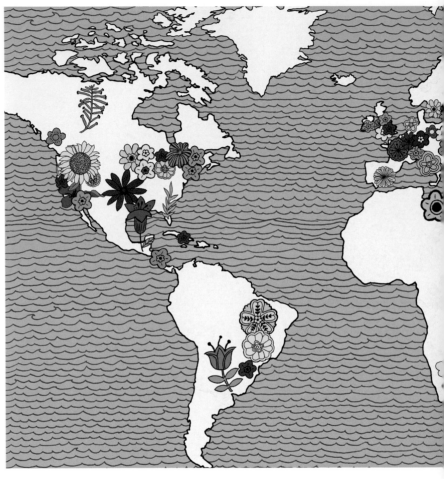

USA
Berkeley, CA
Carmel Valley, CA
Los Angeles, CA
San Diego, CA
San Francisco, CA
Santa Barbara, CA
Santa Cruz, CA
Miami, FL
Chicago, IL
Boston, MA
Detroit, MI
Brooklyn, NY

Bushwick, NY
Delaware County, NY
East New York, NY
New York City, NY
Mansfield, OH
Marietta, OH
Eugene, OR
Portland, OR
Franklin, PA
Warren, PA
Houston, TX
Richmond, VA

CANADA
Alberta, Canada
Montreal, Canada
Toronto, Canada
Vancouver, Canada

LATIN AMERICA
Buenos Aires,
 Argentina
Jardim São Carlos,
 Brazil
Santa Antônio, Brazil
Paraná, Brazil

Tacamiche, Honduras
Tila, Mexico

EUROPE
Vienna, Austria
Brussels, Belgium
Copenhagen, Denmark
Paris, France
Berlin, Germany
Tübingen, Germany
Budapest, Hungary
Debrecen, Hungary
Miskolc, Hungary

GUERRILLA GARDENING
HOT SPOTS OF THE WORLD

Nyiregyhaza, Hungary
Dublin, Ireland
Milan, Italy
Amsterdam, Netherlands
Rotterdam, Netherlands
Granada, Spain
Zurich, Switzerland

UK
Reading, Berks.
High Wycombe, Bucks.
Falmouth, Cornwall
East Portlemouth, Devon

Otterton, Devon
Plymouth, Devon
Torre, Devon
Pentyrch, Glamorgan
Bournemouth, Hants.
Minley Wood, Hants.
Eccles, Lancs.
Standish, Lancs.
Lubenham, Leics.
London
Wellingborough,
  Northants.
Marsden, Oxon.

Crewkerne, Som.
Cobham, Surrey
Woking, Surrey
Singleton, Sussex
Urchfont, Wilts.
Catshill, Worcs.
Huby, Yorks.
Malton, Yorks.

REST OF WORLD
Brisbane, Australia
Sydney, Australia
Guantánamo Bay, Cuba

Mumbai, India
Tokyo, Japan
Nairobi, Kenya
Tripoli, Libya
Bougainville, Papua
  New Guinea
Singapore, Republic
  of Singapore
Johannesburg,
  South Africa
Kagoma, Uganda
Walukumba, Uganda

An Introduction

Four years ago I became a guerrilla gardener. I stepped out into the world to cultivate land wherever I liked. The mission was to fight the miserable public flowerbeds around my neighbourhood.

Until then I had always lived, more or less, on the right side of the law. I had recently moved to a high-rise flat on a bleak roundabout in south London – an area notorious for its labyrinth of pedestrian underpasses, garish pink shopping centre and traffic volumes to rival Britain's busiest motorways. It is the kind of environment that drives people to crime. My crime was gardening on public land without permission and battling whatever was in the way.

Even when one has permission, cultivating a garden is always a fight. We cut back one plant to allow another one to flourish; we scatter seeds, but we rip up weeds and snatch away flowers and fruit before their seed has dispersed. Our gardens are scenes of savage destruction. Animals uproot, frosts cripple, winds topple, rains flood. The guerrilla gardener shares this constant battle with nature with other gardeners. But we have other enemies and ambitions.

This handbook has been compiled from my experience of guerrilla gardening and that of guerrilla gardeners around the world. Radical and reticent, active and retired, successes and failures – they have all shaped these pages. I have also drawn on the documented advice of 'conventional' guerrillas, whose analysis of strategies and tactics can be applicable to our fight. The debate and instruction goes well beyond gardening. To succeed a guerrilla gardener needs to know more. Do not be daunted: read on.

Richard Reynolds
Elephant & Castle, February 2008

TROOP NUMBERS

You will see that most names in this book are followed by numbers. These are their troop numbers, assigned to volunteers when they enlist at GuerrillaGardening.org. Surnames have been omitted because some guerrilla gardeners prefer to remain anonymous. Only guerrilla gardeners who are no longer alive are referred to by their full name.

PART ONE:
THE MOVEMENT

1. A DEFINITION

Picture a garden.

Step into it. Stroll around.

What do you see? Perhaps a riot of tumbling terraces, topiary and pergolas, a cheerful blast of a blooming border or an explosive vegetable patch. Or maybe you are just reminded of the muddy lawn and cracked concrete patio in your garden that resembles a war zone. Whatever garden you are now imagining, it is likely that to one side of it stands a house.

Eschscholzia californica and *Lavandula angustifolia* planted by guerrilla gardeners in central London.

You are picturing a garden as most people see one – as an extension of a home, a landscaped setting to live in, a private space cultivated for the primary pleasure of the permanent occupant. While generous owners permit guests to share their garden, ultimately it is theirs and not yours.*

Over the hill from that garden is another patch of cultivated private space. This one is so big we call it a market garden or farm, and while the owner there may grow strawberries (*Fragaria* x *ananassa*) instead of red roses (*Rosa* 'Super Star') the basic structure is the same: a home and a private garden.

A few readers will have pictured a flowerbed in front of an apartment block or perhaps a lush and leafy park. These are different because the land is publicly accessible. The owner (or whoever is responsible for it) has cultivated the space – perhaps with a bed of primroses (*Primula polyanthus*) or an avenue of lime trees (*Tilia* x *europaea*) – for shared enjoyment. Yet there are limits to this enjoyment. You may survey the scene and sniff the flowers but, as the saying goes, 'take nothing but photographs, leave nothing but footprints and kill nothing but time,' because this is not your garden to tend.

The received opinion is that if you want to be a gardener then you must do so in your own garden or else find a way to be employed or permitted to garden someone else's land.

But some people have a different definition of gardening. I am one of them. I do not wait for permission to become a gardener but dig wherever I see horticultural potential. I do not just tend existing gardens but create them from neglected space. I, and thousands of people like me, step out from home to garden land we do not own. We see opportunities all around us. Vacant lots flourish as urban oases, roadside verges dazzle with flowers and crops are harvested

---

* Horace Walpole observes in his eighteenth-century essay 'On Modern Gardening' that the association between a garden and private ownership has been there from the start: 'Gardening was probably one of the first arts that succeeded to that of building houses, and naturally attended property and individual possession.'

from land that was assumed to be fruitless. In all their forms these have become known as guerrilla gardens. The attacks are happening all around us and on every scale – from surreptitious solo missions to spectacular horticultural campaigns by organized and politically charged cells. This is guerrilla gardening:

THE ILLICIT CULTIVATION
OF SOMEONE ELSE'S LAND.

The battle is gathering pace. Most people own no land. Most of us live in cities and have no garden of our own. We demand more from this planet than it has the space and resources to offer. Guerrilla gardening is a battle for resources, a battle against scarcity of land, environmental abuse and wasted opportunities. It is also a fight for freedom of expression and for community cohesion. It is a battle in which bullets are replaced with flowers (most of the time).

1.1 Little War

Guerrilla is a Spanish word meaning 'little war' – one in which informal combatants make sporadic attacks rather than fighting in great blocks of traditional forces. The first little war of this kind was in 516 BC when the Scythians fought against the invading Persian army of King Darius with nocturnal raids on its supply lines rather than with traditional open field combat.

The g-word was first used to describe the military response to Napoleon Bonaparte's invasion of Spain in 1808. For six years, irregular bands of Spanish fighters attacked the huge occupying imperial French army with little ambushes and civilian agitation. Ordinary men, not trained soldiers, proudly took up arms to defend their country from the invaders and called themselves *guerrilleros*.

Their English allies called them guerrillas. These fighters were well aware of the importance of cultivating someone else's space, though they put this consciousness to a destructive use – they hit the French hard by preventing them from harvesting crops on Spanish soil.

Complementing the Duke of Wellington's campaign, the guerrillas played a major role in the liberation of Spain, and their tactics were soon adopted elsewhere. The Polish uprising against Tsarist Russia in 1863, the American Civil War of the 1860s and the desert attacks in the Middle East by T.E. Lawrence and his men during the First World War were all guerrilla campaigns.

Mao Tse-tung and Che Guevara are two of the best-known guerrillas and both wrote books on the subject. *Yu Chi Chan (On Guerrilla Warfare)* was Mao's 1937 manual, in which he detailed his guerrilla campaigns against the Japanese army in China. Che's *La Guerra de Guerrillas (Guerrilla Warfare)*, written in 1961 after he had successfully overthrown the regime of Fulgencio Batista in Cuba, outlines the principles, structure and tactics of guerrilla warfare. From the mid-1960s, with his handbook as a guide, Che propagated his guerrilla approach in Africa and Latin America as a method of achieving a Marxist revolution.

For these guerrillas, the fight was about more than forcing invaders out of their country – it was about changing society. They had a personal drive. While regular soldiers are trained to be non-political and must trust the motivations behind their commander's orders, guerrillas fight their own little wars. The guerrilla is commander and front-line soldier all in one. It is the self-contained, independent nature of guerrilla fighters that makes their battle so effective. Free from cumbersome bureaucracy and chains of command, a guerrilla is unplugged, off-grid and powered by common sense.

For guerrilla gardeners, as for their military counterparts, a big battle is unnecessary and ineffective: when it comes to war (especially one involving plants), small really is more beautiful.

1.2 The G-Word

Mao and Che's writing and fighting popularized the image of the guerrilla far beyond those on the brink of taking up arms against capitalist or imperial rule. The word was appropriated by a small group of New Yorkers in the early 1970s to describe their illegal gardening on abandoned lots in the East Village. They called themselves the Green Guerillas.

Che and Mao 'guerrilla' merchandising in an Amsterdam street market.

They were aware that the term 'guerrilla' gave their movement a suggestion of exciting rebelliousness. Six years before their dig, in 1967, the most famous guerrilla had been executed, thus becoming a martyr and a poster-prophet in the fight for a more equal society. Che Guevara was, and still is, an inspiration for those setting out to challenge the status quo. His face, made familiar by Alberto Korda's iconic portrait, now stares nobly from thousands of T-shirts. The image conveys the romantic ideal of a guerrilla – confident, piercing eyes surveying the distance; passionate, tight lips and flared nostrils; wild, unkempt hair, tamed by a neat beret. His precise aims and politics are forgotten by most who wear him and instead his one-size-fits-all heroism is celebrated.

Che has become a lovable guerrilla and a marketable commodity. A lot of people want a chunk of Che (even the Church of England and the *Financial Times* have used adaptations of Che's image in their advertising), and all kinds of industries have appropriated the g-word, giving us guerrilla restaurants, guerrilla golf, guerrilla dating and guerrilla tele-sales. But there is usually little that is revolutionary, courageous or heroic about these activities. 'Guerrilla' has become a label to be applied to commercial enterprises, and the result is a loss of potency for the word as a tag. It has become a term for just any kind of unconventional and surprising approach.

Guerrilla gardening, however, is more than this. For a start, guerrilla gardening is not just about breaking convention but about breaking rules. Our enemy is not just normality but something much worse. Just like the original Spanish *guerrilleros*, guerrilla gardeners are reclaiming land from enemy forces, and although our battle is seldom with imperial invaders, as theirs was, it sometimes feels as if we are up against a lot of little Napoleons.

1.3 Guerrillas Gardening

Mao Tse-tung helping Chinese farmers harvest *Gossypium hirsutum*. In reality Mao loved horticultural metaphors more than gardening.

In V. S. Naipaul's acclaimed 1975 novel *Guerrillas*, he describes the garden of a guerrilla fighter called Jimmy Ahmed in the Bahamas. It is the most detailed description of a guerrilla's garden that I know, but the picture is of a place that is dilapidated and unproductive: 'The furrows were full of shiny green weeds; and the ridges, one or two of which showed haphazard, failed planting, were light brown and looked as dry as bone.' The garden eventually becomes the graveyard of Jimmy's English mistress Jane, and his revolution on the island turns rotten.

This unfortunate portrayal of a guerrilla fighter as an uninterested, feeble gardener contrasts with the horticultural inclination of many real guerrillas. Che's motivations for guerrilla warfare in Cuba were about access and rights to land: 'It is tractor and tank at the same time breaking down the walls of the great estate . . . and creating new social relations in the ownership of land.' Emiliano Zapata, an early twentieth-century Mexican guerrilla leader, fought for more equitable distribution of agricultural land, rallying his troops with the cry '*Tierra y libertad*' (land and liberty).

Guerrilla warfare manuals are full of gardening metaphors. Che writes of 'sowing' seeds of revolution and propaganda and reaping the 'fruits of destruction'. When it comes to the nitty-gritty of fighting he acknowledges that 'a group of men in contact with the soil must live from the product of this soil,' but he admits that

guerrillas are better off encouraging local peasants to sow crops, because 'this results in work performed more effectively, with more enthusiasm and skill.' Mao is more encouraging about a guerrilla's skill with plants. 'There is no profound difference between the farmer and the soldier,' he states in his manual. (Although twenty years later he forgot his previous respect for peasant farmers and forced them into communes, triggering the devastating famine of 1959–61. Likewise, his declaration in 1956, 'Let a hundred flowers bloom,' had nothing to do with gardening.)

One guerrilla fighter of recent years showed how a spot of gardening, combined with ecological motivations, can win a war. Francis Ona from the Pacific island of Bougainville described himself as an 'ecological revolutionary'. His fight was against the economic exploitation and environmental degradation of the island of Rio Tinto's Panguna copper mine. Although his first act in 1988 was a violent one – he blew up the mine – he and the Bougainville Revolutionary Army survived the subsequent bloody civil war and decade-long blockade by putting a lot of effort into gardening. They grew food and fuel and were particularly adept with coconuts (*Cocos nucifera*), which powered their vehicles and generators and calmed their curries.

1.4 The Genus

Guerrilla gardening is an organic movement, in the sense that it resembles a living thing.* Like a virulent plant, it has sprung up whenever the environmental conditions of society have been conducive to it. Like seeds blowing from one patch to flower in another near by, guerrilla gardens grow and adapt to local conditions,

---

* The word 'organic' is now also used to mean 'free from artificial fertilizers and pesticides', and while a lot of guerrilla gardening is, this is not exclusively the case.

and in time take on new characteristics, almost like new species of a genus.

The variety of guerrilla gardening disguises it. To me it is rather like the plant genus *Salvia*, of which there are 900 species. Some grow on rocky slopes, others on moist grassland; some bloom with colour, others shy away with muted shades of green; some live for just a year, others grow into mature hardy shrubs. So too guerrilla gardening flourishes in hugely diverse forms all over the planet.

In general both *Salvia* and guerrilla gardening remain on the sidelines of horticulture, while other, more recognizable showy forms take centre stage. Everyone knows that a rose (*Rosa*) is a rose is a rose – even if we do not all garden with them we have all given or received a rose, pinned one to a buttonhole or dropped one into a vase. But not *Salvia*. No, the place of this genus in the garden and in popular culture is relatively obscure, illuminated only occasionally by our appreciation of an individual variety such as the vibrant red 'Scarlet King' (*Salvia splendens*) or the tasty common sage (*Salvia officinalis*).

And so too guerrilla gardening is better known for specific elements within the movement, typically the most outrageous – trees planted on dual carriageways, a dignified statue given a grassy haircut, a large community garden built on derelict land. The more subtle species in the guerrilla gardening genus – the clump of white daffodils (*Narcissus* 'Panache') surreptitiously added to a hedgerow by an imaginative cyclist, the restoration of a neglected flowerbed, the blitzing of a verge with maize (*Zea mays*) – have been overlooked, but they are no less important. Do not underestimate the quiet and modest guerrillas: their gardening can be just as impressive and even more sustainable.

Do not, either, be tempted (as some people have) to describe an activity as *guerrilla* gardening in places where permission has been granted. Defining it as anything other than the *illicit* cultivation of someone else's land belittles the bravery and imagination of genuine

Tulipa 'Isle de France' planted by Lizzie 002, Vicky 2769 and me in East Portlemouth, Devon.

guerrilla gardeners. The most shameless appropriation of the term I have seen was the Mayor of London's brief grassing of Trafalgar Square with Yorkshire turf in May 2007 (a rather pointless, expensive and ecologically dubious gesture about 'greening' the city), which was called 'guerrilla gardening' simply because the small lawn was installed at night.

To some, cultivating land without permission is so straightforward and uncomplicated they have not even considered that what they do is rebellious or that they are a part of a global guerrilla movement. Their approach is encouragement to the rest of us. Like a good botanist, learn to recognize the many varied and true species of the genus. Celebrate and champion guerrilla gardening in its many forms.

1.5 Guerrillas, Not Gorillas

I wonder what you would have imagined had this chapter begun with an invitation to imagine a 'guerrilla garden'? Some would have pictured a jungly space filled with hairy primates or pranksters dressed in fluffy animal costumes. You now know this is wrong. Unfortunately the similarity in sound between 'guerrilla' and 'gorilla' is a problem for anglophone guerrilla gardeners when they describe what they do. Those unfamiliar with our activities see no more reason to associate gardening with guerrillas than with gorillas. The construction of a 'Gorilla Garden' by the London Zoological Society at the world-famous Chelsea Flower Show in 2006 did not help to clarify the definition. Some guerrilla gardeners enjoy the confusion and use grinning, flower-hugging gorillas as a badge for their battalion. Please stop this! While there is a place for witticism within the guerrilla gardening ranks, let's leave gorillas out of it.

2. WHY WE FIGHT

Towards the end of the First World War, Siegfried Sassoon, the soldier-poet who spoke out against the conflict, was told by Winston Churchill, then minister of munitions, 'War is the normal occupation of man.' Sassoon, surprised, asked whether he was really sure about this. Churchill amended his statement: 'War – and gardening.'* I agree, though I think gardening comes more naturally than war. The two are not dissimilar. In both exploits you wrestle forces beyond your control, you shape the landscape and you get messy. There are winners and losers. Both war and gardening are creative as well as destructive. Flower and power go together; they are not

Tending the *Helianthus annuus* in London's urban jungle (a traffic island on Blackfriars Road).

---

* Siegfried Sassoon, *Siegfried's Journey 1916–1920* (Faber and Faber, 1945).

opposites. Fighting and gardening really are quite natural human pastimes, so combining the two involves no great contortion.

If the activity of guerrilla gardening is a natural human instinct, the form it takes certainly varies. We are unified in our actions, cultivating land despite the barriers in our way, but not unified by our objectives or achievements. There is no manifesto to which every guerrilla gardener would happily subscribe – nor should there be. Like guerrillas with guns we have our own motivations, reflecting the environment that we inhabit.

Guerrilla gardeners tend to fall into two groups: those who are driven to beautify space, and those who seek to grow crops in it. (The German language actually allows for this distinction; Germans have *Ziergärten* and *Nutzgärten* – meaning 'ornamental gardens' and 'useful gardens'.) Most guerrilla gardeners in public space are conscious of their role in the community, whether a social benefit is their main aim or just a side-effect of their solo hobby. A guerrilla gardener's work inevitably has an impact on countless people and becomes a powerful form of communication, an expression of the gardener's vision, and sometimes a specific message. The guerrilla gardener in public space reaches out to others and uses plants to draw people in.

2.1 Beautification

I shall not bore on about how beautiful plants are – just go and look at some, smell some, listen to some (or talk to some). They are a gardener's palette, and guerrillas paint with them beyond the edge of the permitted canvas. We spill out, seeing opportunity to splash colour and character all over the place, tagging the landscape, exhibiting in the street – we are graffiti gardeners. Seeing a plant flourish that was nurtured away from home, on someone else's land, in an environment of uncertainty, particularly one that was previously neglected, makes the result more beautiful to my eyes and appealing to my nose than if it had flourished in a sheltered garden. As the Chinese proverb says, 'The flower that blooms in adversity is the most rare and beautiful of all.'

BEAUTIFYING FLOWERBEDS

The potential for beautification of an unloved flowerbed is obvious. I began in this way by rescuing the beds around my tower block, and have moved on to tend others in neglected landmark London locations. At the centre of a roundabout in the shadow of a 300-year-old limestone obelisk on St George's Circus, Southwark, was a neglected elliptical bed containing two shaggy cabbage palms (*Cordyline australis*) and a desert of compacted soil and litter. For two years now, with help from many others, I have transformed it into a thriving herb garden and shrubbery. Two spiky New Zealand flax (*Phormium* 'Firebird') squat at either end of a swathe of small azaleas (*Azalea* 'Johanna'), Michaelmas daisies (*Aster novi-belgii*), heathers of various shades (*Calluna vulgaris*), pittosporum (*Pittosporum tenuifolium* 'Silver Queen'), a bed of lavender (*Lavandula angustifolia*) and rosemary (*Rosmarinus officinalis*) underplanted with tulips (*Tulipa* 'Isle de France'), and a Christmas tree (*Picea abies*).

Ryan 190 struck the tired flowerbeds outside his school in Singapore. At the time he shared a vegetable patch with the fellow members of Victoria Junior College's horticultural club, but gardening there was tedious and unrewarding. In March 2005 he realized that more fun was to be had on a large triangular knoll in front of the school that was covered in a raggedy hedge of bougainvillea (*Bougainvillea* spp.). Ryan hung back after horticultural club meetings to tend it. He cleared weeds and filled in the gaps with cuttings from the other plants and leafy red caladium (*Caladium hortulanum*). Not everything survived, because the ground was

waterlogged and sun-scorched, but bit by bit over a year he added
more plants and his garden flourished. After a year he revealed what
he was up to and had his guerrilla activities legitimized.

Sam 2798 was jogging with his wife near Wicker Park in Chicago
when he noticed a neglected planter in front of a convalescent home.
He soon rounded up some friends, and on the night of 28 August
2006 they struck, hitting the streets with torches round their heads
and a load of juniper bushes (*Juniperus communis*), variegated feather
grass (*Calamagrostis* x *acutiflora*) and a flowering pink potentilla
(*Potentilla nitida*). They topped up the thin earth with 70 kilos of new
soil and dug in assorted perennials donated by a local plant store, all
of which greatly cheered up the spectating convalescents.

BEAUTIFYING EMPTY SPACE

Where there has never been colour a guerrilla gardener finds a way
to bring it into the environment, seeing potential where others saw
blank, barren boredom. A bare yard, a dull street, a bald roundabout
and a derelict lot all offer opportunity.

Angela 2585 and friends targeted a scrappy roundabout on Viale
Umbria in Milan. Someone had planted it with a new tree, but this
stood lonely among grass and litter. She remodelled the site with a
bed round the tree, planting lavender (*Lavandula angustifolia*), box
trees (*Buxus sempervirens*) and a scattering of alpine flower seeds.

In San Diego, Ava 949 seed-bombed a ten-mile stretch of
Imperial Avenue (a thoroughfare not as grand as it sounds) by
lobbing self-contained fertile projectiles out from her car window.
In New York, Peter 509 filled the median planter that runs down
Houston Street with daffodils (*Narcissus* 'King Alfred') to give
drivers waiting at the junction something pleasant to look at. The
bulbs were donated by Hans van Waardenburg, a Dutch bulb
supplier who pledged to give New York half a million bulbs every
year to commemorate 9/11. Peter also built planters around trees

along Houston Street without permission. Bright wooden boxes went in the place of the trees' rampant litter-trapping suckers. Even without plants in them Peter sees the containers as public art, and he painted them blue with white clouds on, to which (to his delight) taggers added their own graffiti. They stayed in place for two years until they were removed to make way for the redevelopment of neighbouring buildings and the sidewalk. Peter's grand dream is of a long roadside garden – a twisting ribbon that weaves together the green pockets of New York's gardens.

Nisha 3057 is a yoga teacher in Mumbai who finds beauty and calm by guerrilla gardening in this densely populated city. She plants trees, which she describes as giving a feeling of stability and grounding as well as the practical benefits of shade and fruit – all hugely beneficial in a manic, tropical city. In 1999, she sneaked into the communal space of her housing society home and planted a gulmohar (*Delonix regia*) with beautiful orange flowers, a canary-yellow copper pod (*Peltophorum pterocarpum*), a sacred ashoka tree* (*Saraca asoca*) and a wonderful drought-resistant, medicinal neem tree (*Azadirachta indica*). She later employed a gardener as a mercenary guerrilla by paying him to water them for her, and as time went on she watched the trees flourish and won support from members of the housing society when they were threatened with the saw.

Some of the most celebrated guerrilla gardens were planted on vacant lots, usually where a building once stood or a road was to be expanded. It takes a brave gardener to transform a pile of rubble and, typically, piles of junk into a blooming garden, but the satisfaction is immense, and the garden that emerges is one that not only looks beautiful but can be of a scale to provide many other benefits, particularly space for a community to come together. Donald 277 and Adam 276 showed me around the magnificent

---

* Lord Buddha was born under an ashoka and the Hindus dedicate this tree to Kama Deva, the God of Love.

community gardens they tend in New York which had illicit origins, and Julia 013 toured me around younger ones of a similar scale in Berlin. These are just some of countless beautiful spaces built out of waste ground, and their stories will be told later on.

BEAUTIFYING BEYOND

Guerrilla gardeners' ambitions are not always limited to a defined flowerbed, tub or abandoned lot. Some spread their beautification in less defined drifts, letting nature and chance play more of a role. Roadside verges are particularly suitable for beautifying in this way.* Lucy 579, an artist and illustrator in south London and self-proclaimed 'fairy spreading magic dust', scatters wildflower seeds with abandon. She rarely leaves the house in spring without a pocketful of seeds to sprinkle. Her main target has been the nearby railway station at Hither Green where she scattered seeds on waste ground strewn with discarded snack food. She describes her station now as 'Dog Daisy Heaven', a place where she can pick a flower for her hair in the morning before the commuter crush. Thomas 347, from Davenport in Delaware County, has lined the road that passes through his town with daylilies (*Hemerocallis fulva*). Denise 183 thought that the new motorway embankments of the M42 in Worcestershire were dull and brightened them up by planting daffodil bulbs (*Narcissus pseudonarcissus*).

Guerrilla gardeners do not restrict their horticultural aspirations to the ground. When Helen 1106 walks around London she looks up and imagines a romantic alternative metropolis. She described to me her vision of a landscape of towering buildings covered with

---

* Perhaps the best-known scatterer of flower seeds is Miss Rumphius in the 1982 children's story of that name by Barbara Cooney. Inspired by the blue and purple lupins (*Lupinus angustifolius*) seeding naturally beyond her garden, she fills her pockets with seeds and wanders over fields and headlands, highways and country lanes, around the schoolhouse and the back of the church, and into hollows and along stone walls. The reader turns the page and sees lupins everywhere.

vegetation rather than glossy glass and steel. She has begun her mission by planting a little ivy (*Hedera helix*) in nooks and crannies near the Bank of England where it is unlikely to be discovered (at least for a while).* Also in London, Gordon 2888 has hung baskets off empty hooks near Oxford Circus, and Sean 2350, despite being blind, has trained climbers up the telegraph pole and along the cable outside his house in Kentish Town.

One of Poster Child 3261's flower boxes filled with *Celosia plumosa* on Augusta Avenue, Toronto.

The more you think about guerrilla gardening, the more potential locations will become apparent. Train your eye and you will see the landscape in a totally new and exciting way.

2.2 Food

One excellent reason for cultivating someone else's land without their permission is hunger. At its most urgent, guerrilla gardening is about people fighting for the right to have dinner on their plate.

GARDENING OUT OF NECESSITY

Bloody battles have been fought by guerrilla gardeners for a place to grow food. In the 1970s, thousands of landless Mexicans seized hundreds of thousands of hectares of agricultural land. They named their first stronghold Campamento Emiliano Zapata, after their long-gone guerrilla hero, and campaigned, sometimes violently, for more space to garden. President Echeverría granted them permission to hold on to some land, assigning them 100,000 hectares in 1976, but the guerrilla gardeners wanted more and seized another 600,000 hectares. Eventually the Mexican regime could no longer tolerate the advance of the guerrilla gardeners and took back much of the

---

* Planting ivy as a guerrilla gardener is controversial and risky, since a vigorous one can cause damage to the building's façade. Using it is tantamount to planting a bomb with a very long fuse.

land, killing a hundred people in the process. A more recent example is the fight of the Tacamiches in Honduras to make use of an abandoned banana plantation. Between 1995 and 2001 they illegally cultivated land and battled against bulldozers, bureaucracy and big banana business, eventually winning the right to continue.

These are a few of countless examples, not all of which have been bloody. In Brazil, the MST, or Movement of Landless Rural Workers,* helps people to take unused land peacefully, grow their own food and establish sustainable communities. Seizing the land has been a successful strategy for later gaining legitimization, and since 1985 the organization has managed to win land titles for more than 350,000 families. In South Africa, the Landless People's Movement is campaigning for access to agricultural resources for the country's 28 million poor and the legalizing of illegal occupations of unused land.

Hundreds of years ago in the history of guerrilla gardening it was the same basic need to grow food that galvanized people into action. Rising food prices and unemployment, combined with ample waste ground and a strong sense of injustice, motivated Gerrard Winstanley and his band of Diggers to cultivate St George's Hill in Surrey in 1649. Other guerrilla gardeners soon mobilized in Wellingborough, Northamptonshire. 'We have spent all we have; our trading is decayed; our wives and children cry for bread; our lives are a burden to us,' wrote Richard Smith and associates in *A Declaration by the Diggers of Wellingborough* (1650).

The fight for food is by no means restricted to massive guerrilla gardening armies or campaigning groups. It is usually very informal.

---

* MST (Movimento dos Trabalhadores Rurais Sem Terra) is a powerful organization largely funded by small contributions from members. It operates 30 radio stations, a national newspaper, three banks, a school for leadership training, two meat-storage plants, a milk-packing facility and a coffee-roasting company. Since 1995 it has also hosted an 'Agrarian Reform Olympics' which has included 1,500 athletes from 23 squatted settlements. Visit mstbrazil.org.

Anders 860 has written about how median strips between busy highways in Kenya are planted by squatters near by as miniature plots of maize (*Zea mays*).* Mama Afuwa 3187 lives near Kagoma, Uganda, and rents a small bungalow. She has no land, but when Lyla 1046, a guerrilla gardener from London, visited her she was shown a fine crop of onions (*Allium cepa*) planted on the common scrub beside her home. Elsewhere in Uganda Lyla came across all sorts of subsistence guerrilla gardening. Land set aside for road expansion is illegally planted with maize (*Zea mays*), and in Walukumba guerrilla gardeners inhabit the residential districts of one of the largest industrial estates in East Africa: the industry is long gone and the largely unemployed residents make do by growing matooke (*Musa* x *paradisiac*) in the common ground. They were nervous to talk to Lyla about it because the government has been hassling them to tidy up.

Growing food is a hugely uplifting experience. It can be a spiritual as well as edible antidote to an otherwise debilitating environment. Detainees in Guantánamo Bay have been guerrilla gardening as a diversion from their incarceration. One of them is Saddiq 754, a Uighur from Afghanistan, who has been held in the Camp Iguana section since 2002. He built his garden in the grounds of the prison by softening the sun-baked soil with water at night and gradually scratching away at it with a plastic spoon until he had enough soil to plant seeds saved from meals. He and fellow inmates have grown watermelon, peppers, garlic, cantaloupe and even a tiny lemon plant. Saddiq's lawyer had regularly pressed the Joint Task Force Guantánamo to build the prisoners a garden, but they had refused. He was astonished to hear that Saddiq had just gone ahead anyway.

* Anders Corr, *No Trespassing* (South End Press, 1999).

GARDENING FOR SELF-SUFFICIENCY

Reducing dependency on large supermarkets and eating food you know to be healthy are powerful incentives to grow your own. Inspiration comes from all manner of fascinating sources: the ancient urban food systems of the Aztec civilization, the medieval urban agro-ecosystem of the Marais in Paris, the wartime Liberty and Victory Gardens* in the US and the Dig for Victory campaign in Britain, the co-operative urban farms of blockaded Cuba, the loose philosophical design system of permaculture, and more recently the American architect Fritz Haeg's Edible Estates initiative. Many people are interested in growing food – in Britain vegetable seed sales are now outstripping flower seeds for the first time since the Second World War. But in theory you can only grow your own if you have land of your own; or you can turn to guerrilla gardening.

There is another option for the guerrilla gardener who wants a crop but has no land to grow it on, which is perhaps best described as guerrilla harvesting. I am not talking about stealing – pinching vegetables is a step too far towards criminality for most guerrilla gardeners – but there is a middle ground. Just as some cultivate wasteland, others harvest waste crops. Californians David 1992, Matias 1993 and Austin 1994 are a collective who go by the name of 'Fallen Fruit' and through their website (FallenFruit.org) encourage people to harvest fruit trees in public spaces. They have mapped their neighbourhood of Silver Lake, Los Angeles, marking where accessible fresh fruit is going spare, including trees growing in public as well as branches hanging into the street from private gardens. They now campaign for more fruit trees to be grown in public and for private gardeners to put them on their perimeter,

---

* During the First World War the Liberty Gardens involved 5% of Americans. About 5,285,000 gardens produced 8% of the nation's gross value in agricultural commodities. During the Second World War the Victory Gardens, at their peak in 1944, produced 42% of the country's fresh vegetables.

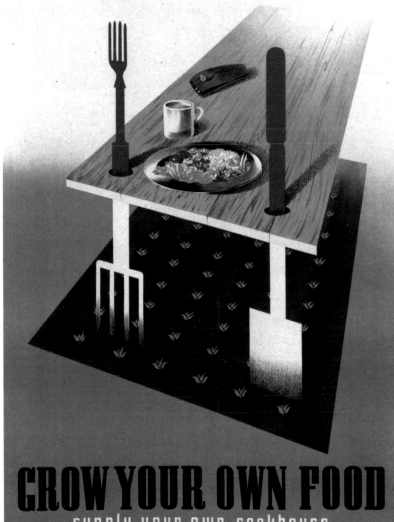

...every available piece of land must be cultivated

GROW YOUR OWN FOOD
supply your own cookhouse

so that cities can have a local, accessible and informal supply of snack food.

Guerrilla gardeners have proudly shown me their crops. Hans 1287 in Berlin has a broad patch of leafy vegetables, lettuces (*Lactuca sativa* 'Lollo Rosso'), cabbages (*Brassica oleracea* 'Capitata Group') and kale (*Brassica oleracea* 'Acephala Group'). In New York, Adam 276 plucked me a sweet red pepper (*Capsicum annuum*), and Johanna 2491 toured me around her impressive herb garden brimming with all sorts of different mint (*Mentha* spp.) and enormous marrows (*Cucurbita pepo*). Although spaces away from the traffic fumes are preferable, Bill 2787 has sowed pole beans (*Phaseolus vulgaris*) along a fence between Telegraph and West Outer Drive on the roadside verge of Interstate 96 in Detroit, and I have had a clump of bright yellow Swiss chard (*Beta vulgaris* var. *cicla*) flourishing in my patch near the bus stops of Elephant & Castle in London.

GARDENING AND IDEALISM

Growing edible crops on someone else's land does not need to be just for sustenance; in places where food is ample, accessible and cheap, guerrilla gardeners may do so for more idealistic reasons. For many it is a symbolic gesture, demonstrating that there is a more sustainable way to live than relying on agribusiness. Ecological and political motivations are increasingly important for guerrilla gardeners, even if most do not describe themselves as eco-warriors.

Anders 860 helped found the Santa Cruz Union of the Homeless and in 1992 occupied a piece of wasteland owned by the State of California. Although the police closed down their tented encampment after a few days, their guerrilla gardening continued. In his book *No Trespassing* he tells how for five years they grew vegetables, and twice a week the activist group Food Not Bombs served free meals to the homeless. The garden was destroyed in 1997 and replaced with a pathway to Toys R Us and Circuit City.

More recently, Justin 734 and friends have been turning vacant lots in San Francisco into productive gardens. His first was a four-and-a-half-acre plot at the foot of Bernal Heights that in the mid-1990s had been a farm run by the San Francisco League of Urban Gardeners. The organization had collapsed and the land was neglected, so Justin chose to remedy the situation by guerrilla gardening. He and his troops arrived with a rotovator and compost to put the land back into food production. This demonstration of interest and effort soon convinced the city authorities to sanction the reclaiming of Alemany Farm (AlemanyFarm.org), which is the city's only urban farm. Organic food is distributed among the volunteers and families from the neighbouring subsidized housing community.

David 1168 and Michael 1169 are graphic designers in Tokyo, the biggest city in the world with a population of 34 million. They are also guerrilla gardeners with a passion for growing food. They began in 2005 by chucking pumpkin (*Cucurbita maxima*) seeds into a vacant lot near David's home. These did well, so they continued with a small guerrilla farm in the Kamiyacho district on waste ground behind an office block. They have planted broccoli (*Brassica oleracea* 'Italica Group') in small holes outside the Yokohama Civic Art Gallery, and daikon radishes (*Raphanus sativus longipinnatus*) in tree pits. This is a gesture towards sustainable agriculture, and a way of giving away free food. 'It's about living in an edible jungle,' says David. 'Vegetables are best fresh, and so I thought they should be grown locally.'

Even small-scale horticultural acts can be powerful gestures. In Crewkerne, Somerset, Ben 2676 demonstrated the potential for a more productive landscape by successfully growing maize (*Zea mays*) in a shabby planter two metres square right outside the main entrance of his local supermarket with the help of his young daughters Lily 2677 and Noor 2678.

GARDENING FOR STIMULATION

Guerrilla gardeners also grow crops that are more intoxicating than vegetables. In the global drug trade this activity is a cottage industry compared with mass-market drug agribusinesses, and there are advantages to the guerrilla's boutique approach. A problem for drug barons who grow narcotics on their own land is that their incriminating crop is rooted to their land's title deed, so they require a personal security force to keep prying enforcement agencies away – Peru's coca growers rely on the 500-strong guerrilla army called the Shining Path for protection. But guerrilla gardeners need no guerrilla army because they are not cultivating their own land; as long as they are not caught in the act there is nothing to link them to the evidence.

One anonymous guerrilla gardener discreetly planted 3,400 marijuana (*Cannabis sativa* subsp. *indica*) seedlings along the riverbanks of Carmel Valley, in the grounds of a huge Californian estate owned by the media baron Rupert Murdoch. They were eventually spotted, but the guerrilla gardener escaped before he could be arrested and the crops were destroyed. Less industrious but even more blatant drug cultivation occurred in the picturesque German town of Tübingen. Severin 888 planted cannabis (*Cannabis sativa* subsp. *sativa*) seeds in the town's numerous colourful flowerbeds, which survived periodic civic weeding to grow into mature plants.

Severin 888's cannabis flourishes in a civic planter in Tübingen, Germany.

2.3 Community

The benefit of green community spaces in cities is seldom disputed. Transplanting a country-like environment to the city 'can always instil a hallowed calm, a spirit of reverence into the mind and heart of man', according to the nineteenth-century radical social reformer Francis Place, and his aspirations are still shared today.

Guerrilla gardeners
and friends
picnic in the Rosa
Rose Garden in
Friedrichshain,
Berlin.

The vogue for building public parks in early Victorian Britain was hailed as an antidote to the ills of industrial society. City parks were not just a breath of fresh air: they were considered a potential cure for drunkenness. John Loudon, who designed one of the first of these public parks, said that his Arboretum was there to 'give the people of Derby an opportunity to learn botany, to enjoy the pure air of the park as an alternative to the debasing pursuits and brutalizing pleasures of drinking and cock fighting'. Parks were there to pacify a potentially rebellious society, and some even included an outlet for political debate – Victoria Park in East London had a forum specifically for political meetings.

While some new parks are created today, the agenda is more often geared towards flagship projects rather than smaller community spaces where people need them. A visit to a park is marketed as an event, whereas many would prefer to have a place to pop out to. Ambitious guerrilla gardeners fight for the right to have a space that can serve the community in this way. Zachary 922, a Green Guerilla in New York, brims with fervour and speaks for many when he says, 'It is our right and duty to retake that land so that it serves the needs of the neighbourhood. There are very few places in this city or country where people can come together without paying money, do not have to buy a drink to sit there, can come and go as they please, garden, build art or just socialize, have a barbecue and be in a positive space, not a concrete box, learn stuff, get job skills, just getting their hands in the dirt.'

The passion for seizing community garden space is also felt in territories that are much more hostile to community gardens than New York. A new one has sprung up recently in the archetypal Middle England town of Reading. In the shabby Katesgrove district, just off the deep-cut dual carriageway of the Inner Distribution Road, Stuart 1952, a 22-year-old painter and decorator, led a team of guerrilla gardeners in creating the Common Ground Community

Garden on some neglected waste ground next to a squat. They cleared a large area of needles, used condoms and broken glass and replaced it with a small lawn, wood chippings, seats hewn from logs and pots of purple petunias (*Petunia* x *hybrida*).

With his altruistic motives Stuart reached out very publicly to the community, inviting them to enjoy the reclaimed space with an inaugural barbecue. This news alerted Reading borough council, who intervened and issued the guerrillas with an injunction on the grounds of 'health and safety', an excruciatingly ironic claim given the awful state the land was in before – on the council's watch. The barbecue carried on regardless, 200 people came, and the guerrillas set about fighting a legal battle for the right to continue, rallying support from the local media with press releases. They were summoned to the magistrates' court and took their campaign there with the slogan 'Defend the Community, Defend the Garden'. The garden was still looking splendid when I visited late in August 2007, but Stuart and his team continue to face legal battles to be allowed to continue.

For those guerrilla gardeners who choose to fight with others, there are additional benefits – including the camaraderie of warfare. Frauke 242 in Berlin is a guerrilla gardener who sees community as critical to making a space successful. I spent a summer's evening with her and other troops, lounging around an alfresco three-piece living-room suite built from turf. After a bit of electric grass trimming we made ourselves comfortable and talked about why this had been illicitly built on a desolate piece of industrial waste ground. It was a gesture, she said, to raise awareness of what the land should be, which is an official extension of the neighbouring Mauerpark. Its construction had been promised but then stalled because of wranglings about the land's ownership.

Frauke supports the park but is keener on community gardens that involve people in their creation. 'Everything happens through the community. That means exchange, learning from one another, self-organization, ecological aspects, waste reduction – do I have to own it or is it enough to be able to use it?' In Berlin she now has permission to garden some areas with the community, carrying out a public service that the city cannot afford to pay for.

Outside a community garden the rest of the neighbourhood benefits as well: the positive impact extends down the street, like the fragrance of its flowers. A well-tended community garden, occupied at all hours of the day by someone wielding a heavy implement, makes a positive contribution to reducing crime. Adam 276 walked me around Hells Kitchen in New York, and described how drug-dealing and prostitution have been reduced in what was an insalubrious neighbourhood, partly as a result of the Clinton Community Garden. The hustlers, johns and panhandlers have lost their 'turf' (which was actually just tarmac at that time).

President Roosevelt appreciated the power of nature to unify communities. In 1945 he hosted an inaugural session of the United Nations in the Cathedral Grove of the magnificent Muir Woods, a forest of towering redwoods (*Sequoia sempervirens*) just outside San Francisco. He felt that, whatever our backgrounds, we should share a respect for the power of nature, especially giant trees several thousand years old. On a similar theme, Edie 1660 in New York wonders: 'Perhaps we should get Homeland Security money to build community gardens: it is a great way to integrate communities together.'

2.4 Health

Just as the health of the community benefits from a garden, so the individuals involved reap rewards too. The physical advantages are well known: gardening of any kind burns calories, while trimming a hedge tones biceps, and digging and squatting both help to shape thighs and buttocks. The health benefits of gardening were identified by Dr Daniel Schreber of Leipzig during the nineteenth century. He envisaged green areas in the city for the poor's children, though it was not until after his death that the idea began to flourish.* Similar to British allotments, but founded with the specific aim of improving the health of those living in industrial cities, 'Schrebergärten' grew popular during periods of national crisis and are still enjoyed today.

Gardening is good exercise. You need not pound away in a brightly lit, air-conditioned gymnasium or pay to pitch up for a communal sporting activity – and you will have something to show for your effort not only when you look in the mirror but also when you survey the landscape. The sweat-inducing work of clearing a neglected patch and digging the hard-baked soil for the first time is particularly effective. Troops who have guerrilla-gardened with me say 'Give me the hoe' and flay away happily at the ground. These gardeners often admit that they have no interest in plants; they just like to dig and get sweaty. Gardening is a cheap alternative to the gym and safer than extreme sports.

For Dr Schreber, the activity of gardening and the associated physical exercise was one route to a healthy mind and body for the individual and by extension to a healthier society. More recently, Dr Roger Ulrich of Texas University demonstrated that hospital patients who had a view of a tree outside their window recovered more quickly after surgery than patients without one. You do not even need to lift a trowel – gardens are healthy for everybody.

Gardening is also good for the head. Edie 1660 describes how several New York community gardeners have serious mental illnesses. 'People who would not quite function can become really powerful in the gardens,' she says with delight. I think guerrilla gardening is even better for those with a tendency towards occasional

---

* Dr Schreber (1808–61) was also a paediatrician. Although his approach to raising plants is still widely commended, his authoritarian approach to rearing children is now considered to be tantamount to abuse.

bouts of mania. The subject of mental health came up quite unprompted in my conversations with several guerrilla gardeners who related how their activity had helped them through a particularly difficult time or stabilized their moods. The exercise and the extra passion and sense of adventure you need to guerrilla-garden definitely suits the mildly unhinged. While you do not need to be mad to be a guerrilla gardener, a little craziness definitely helps, and guerrilla gardening seems to help temper that madness too.

Guerrilla gardening is also a way of doing a little bit for the health of Earth – in short, more plants means more carbon absorption, more productive landscapes and cooler climates. Paul 2207, a photographer who flies around the world documenting environmental degradation, has turned to guerrilla tree-planting to compensate for his heavy emissions. When he is at home in the Welsh countryside he hops fences to surreptitiously add oak saplings (*Quercus rober*) to farmers' copses. Yes, it would take much more than this to eradicate his carbon footprint entirely, but taking the time to plant trees and look after them is certainly better medicine for his guilty conscience than sending an easy payment to a carbon neutralizing company.

2.5 Business

There is a commercial benefit of making an area more attractive. As a rule of thumb, well-kept areas tend to be more prosperous. Where people can afford to spend the time and money making their environment more attractive, their efforts in turn encourage others to visit, live and spend their money there, making further beautification possible. Shrewd homeowners and retailers should look beyond their property and consider improving the landscape in which they sit because it is good for business. Profit is a strong motivation for battle.

I came across Buster 1266's guerrilla gardening in a rural lay-by near Singleton, deep in the Sussex countryside. He runs a mobile snack van by the roadside and to earn a living he needs cars to slow down and consider stopping for fast food. Rather than emblazon his white wagon with dazzling notices he has jazzed up the roadside verge with colour. When trade is slow he takes out his strimmer and carves a small lawn out of the undergrowth which he has edged with pansies (*Viola tricolor*), providing a little piece of manicured suburbia for his customers to enjoy while they eat his bacon butties. Likewise in Brussels I met Mario 2506 who had planted sunflowers (*Helianthus annuus*) in tree pits outside his second-hand clothes shop on Rue Lesbroussart.

It is not just independent traders who use guerrilla gardening to boost business. Advertising agencies have added it to their marketing weaponry as a stunt with ecologically positive overtones. In Hungary, Alex 1848, creative director of Raygun, used it to promote the Hegyalja music festival. He devised an elaborate synchronized strike across the country. On 4 June 2007 four teams of ten local people in Nyireghaza, Debrecen, Miskolc and Budapest hit the ground at precisely 9pm and planted over a thousand flowers in prominent locations. These included petunias (*Petunia* 'Pearly Wave') and tobacco plants (*Nicotiana alata*). The day after the music festival, the organizer came forward to take public responsibility for the action and the story was reported positively across the country.

I have heard guerrilla gardeners scoff at commercial motivation, but I advise everyone to be conscious of it. Beautifying public space has a gentrifying effect, whether intended or not. Duncan 197, a guerrilla gardener in Woking, Surrey, noticed how his illicit patch delighted an estate agent whom he spotted lining up his camera to ensure the bed of sixty dwarf daffodils (*Narcissi* 'Tête-à-tête') on a shabby roundabout were included in the foreground of a neighbour's property advertisement. Not quite what Duncan had in mind.

Ultimately, beautifying your neighbourhood may actually threaten the permanence of your garden. The improvements that guerrilla gardeners brought to the rough neighbourhoods of 1970s New York contributed to the increasing value of the land and the possibility of their being reclaimed by the disinterested landowner. This unfortunate side-effect nagged me as I tended the neglected flowerbeds below my rented tower block flat. With every dig of my shovel I was pushing up the prices of the adjacent properties and making it more difficult to get my foot on the property ladder. My home-owning neighbours were of course delighted and among the most encouraging.

But knowing this did not stop me. I would rather rent and live in an attractive environment that I can garden than own a property in a slum and stay indoors.

2.6 Expression

Gardening is a vivid form of expression. Doing it in public, on land that is not yours, sends an even stronger message. Society needs this kind of creativity.

You might find yourself living in a beautiful house with a beautiful garden in a beautiful neighbourhood with all the comforts and food you could want. This is the popular image of an ideal city, perhaps one reinvigorated by Olympic investment or built from scratch in a desert – all manicured perfection and efficient amenities, and a personality or image that fits neatly on a postcard. Yet scratch the surface and this is hollow and unfulfilling. The smaller details of public places that give a place personality are being erased by globalized commerce and globalized landscape architecture, planning rules and codes of conduct. Public space is increasingly anodyne – the role of people, our role, is expected to mimic that of the stick men glued to an architect's model. We are inert decoration, only allowed to spend time in public space if we have money to spend there too.

But why should our role in this space be so controlled? My local shopping centre recently even banned people from wearing hoods indoors.* As guerrilla gardeners we do not just want to walk past someone else's attractive flowerbeds: we want to shape that landscape and use plants to talk to people in some way.

THE MESSAGE OF GARDENING

At its simplest, the message is about the potential for creating beauty and productivity in the landscape. Becky 735, when describing the Alemany Farm Project in San Francisco, says the goal is not just to grow food but also to 'inspire, educate and empower San Franciscans about the possibilities, benefits and techniques of growing food in our own city'.

Heather 1986 is a landscape architect of large corporate projects who turned to guerrilla gardening in her spare time to express herself in ways that her day job did not permit. She fell in with the Bitter Melon Council (BitterMelon.org), a group dedicated to celebrating this acerbic-tasting, warty-looking and unpopular plant. So, on National Bitter Melon Day in 2005, Heather assembled a stall in Boston's Chinatown and handed out the materials to make bitter melon seed bombs.

The kit included directions to bomb some nearby neglected land that could be treated in a sympathetic, homeopathic way – 'bitter land with bitter medicine', as she told me. To enrich the act with even more symbolism, along with the melon seeds she handed out paper napkins so that the guerrilla gardeners could write down

---

* Clothing regulations are not a new problem. In 1846 Peel Park in Salford opened to the public with a great celebration, but the fun was curtailed in 1868 when a new by-law stipulated that visitors had to be dressed in clean and decent clothes.

something that made them bitter, and fire this away together with the bitter melon seed. Unfortunately, many of the Chinese people appreciated the free bitter melon seeds so much that they had no intention of discarding them where they were unlikely to be able to harvest, so they took the seeds home to grow in private.

Some guerrilla gardeners have told me how they want their spaces to be living museums of plants and wildlife for children to learn about animals, the origin of food and the rhythm of seasons – messages from which city dwellers have become detached. A good example of such a place is Berlin's Kinderbauernhof Mauerplatz (the Mauerplatz Children's Farmstead) in Kreuzberg on Leuschnerdamm. A group of mothers began their guerrilla activity in March 1981 on a deserted patch within the vicinity of the Berlin Wall. Today, signs explain where plants come from around the world, children play with the ponies, and a group of Turkish immigrants are able to continue their rural traditions in the foreign environment of Germany's capital city.

PLANTING A MEMORIAL

A garden's colour and cheerfulness transforms the spirit of a landscape that has become associated with tragedy. No one asks permission to place a wreath of cut flowers in a plastic wrapper by the roadside; I do not think anyone needs to ask permission to make the same gesture with a living plant.

Driving through Hampshire, Stephen 1337 noticed a neglected roundabout on a stretch of the A327 passing by Minley Wood, near where the body of murdered teenager Milly Dowler was found in 2002. He wanted to cheer the place up, so working alone with a fluorescent jacket as disguise he dug in a sack of mixed daffodils (*Narcissus* spp.). It was all done in twenty frantic minutes, but he tells me it has lightened the sombre mood of the place. Virginia 501 from Houston wrote to me saying that she and her children would be planting sunflowers (*Helianthus annuus*) by the roadside where her husband was killed a few months before. They chose to guerrilla-garden on his birthday.

Paul 1119 has used guerrilla gardening to mark hundreds of memorials in a continuing and powerful art project spread across England and the USA. He began in Manchester, planting pansies (*Viola x wittrockiana*) to mark where homophobic attacks had taken place ('pansy' being a slang term for a gay man in anglophone countries).

Using police records of where both verbal and physical attacks had occurred, Paul planted the pansies along pavements, in crevices beneath trees, at the foot of walls and to plug gaps in flowerbeds. He took a photo of each one and named the image after the particular abuse that had occurred there. '*Faggots! . . . Poofs! . . . Queers!*' is a beautiful burgundy pansy on Oxford Road outside Sainsbury's supermarket; '*It's about time we went gay-bashing again, isn't it?*' is a pale peachy one that is timidly growing through some melting snow on Grosvenor Street. The Pansy Project went legal when Paul sought and won the support of cultural institutions in North America and Britain, and it now has its own website (ThePansyProject.com).

In March 2007 Paul was given funding by the London Lesbian and Gay Film Festival to plant along Queen's Walk on the South Bank to mark the murder in 2004 of David Morley, which was widely perceived to have been motivated by homophobia. As well as filling empty tree pits and flowerbeds, pansies were stuffed into ribbons of soggy black stockings and bin liners to be wrapped temporarily around the bases of bins and bollards.

Paul asked me to help clear away this temporary part of the exhibition and transplant the pansies somewhere permanent. And so I spent an evening with Claire 1971, Lyla 1046 and Gavin 2881 crawling around the South Bank prising out pansies and perplexing

the rowdy al fresco drinkers who favoured us with some light horticultural abuse.

SAY IT WITH SUNFLOWERS

A guerrilla gardening project that encapsulates many different aspects of why we fight is the sunflower planting begun by Girasol 829 in Brussels. In spring 2006, he and three friends who he met at art school conceived the activity as something collaborative to do outside their day jobs. From the outset they wanted the project to link and shape both the physical landscape and the online landscape. They decided to plant sunflowers (*Helianthus annuus*) all over the city and to encourage other people to do the same around the world. They would do so under the 'Brussels Farmer' name.

For Girasol, giant sunflowers were the perfect plant to use. Not only would they be hugely visible within a short space of time, easy to photograph for the virtual-meets-real aspect of their art project, and easy and cheap to plant; they are also richly symbolic. On the Brussels Farmer website (Brussels-Farmer.blogspot.com) his manifesto describes how sunflowers are an antidote to the problems within cities – their colour and wide faces induce positive feelings, their seeds can be used for environmentally friendly bio-diesel and bird feed, and they are versatile and fairly self-sufficient. Beauty, productivity, community and a great deal of optimism are expressed by this project.

In 2007 he declared 1 May *Journée internationale de la guérilla tournesol* (International Sunflower Guerrilla Day), and encouraged co-ordinated guerrilla acts in Bordeaux, Paris, Eindhoven and London. It is a day that I hope will continue to be celebrated.

To artists and philosophers, guerrilla gardening is to be championed. Creativity as social act was described as the ultimate objective for the Situationist International movement. Writing in 1956, the Dutch artist Constant Nieuwenhuys imagined a civilization,

Viola x wittrockiana planted on London's South Bank by Paul 1119 as a memorial to David Morley, who was murdered here.

New Babylon, in which man became free from producing things and so, aided by easy travel and efficient telecommunications, he was free to play and create all day long – thinking man became playful man: *Homo ludens*.

One of the many *Helianthus annuus* planted to mark 1 May, International Sunflower Guerrilla Day, celebrated by guerrilla gardeners around the world.

More of us are 'at play' today than ever before, but only guerrilla gardeners are truly living the situationist utopian vision. For, as Nieuwenhuys wrote in a 1974 exhibition catalogue, New Babylonians wander 'without the passivity of tourists, but fully aware of the power they have to act upon the world, to transform it, recreate it. At any given moment in his creative activity, the New Babylonian is himself in direct contact with his peers. Each one of his acts is public, each one acts on a milieu which is also that of the others and elicits spontaneous reactions.' (Whatever that means.)

The old Babylon* of Mesopotamia is famous as home to one of the seven wonders of the ancient world: the spectacular Hanging Gardens of Babylon. These are now gone, but I encourage you to create awe-inspiring gardens of the imaginary New Babylon – wherever you are.

* Buried underground 85km south of Baghdad, Iraq.

3. WHAT WE FIGHT

Most guerrilla gardeners are up against two main enemies. These are not people or organizations but two conditions of the landscape: *scarcity* and *neglect*, problems that come from how we all use the land. They are in some ways contradictory – if land is scarce you would not expect it to be neglected, and likewise in an area where land is being neglected you would expect there to be plenty to spare. But the world is not logical. People are not distributed according to what they need from the landscape, and rules and regulations prevent those who want land from making use of neglected space.

Guerrilla gardeners ignore the rules and regulations, resolve the contradiction and have a lot of fun doing it. By cultivating someone else's land without their permission, a guerrilla gardener

The expansive and immaculate lawns outside the United Nations building in Manhattan are out of bounds. What a greedy waste of space.

directly confronts the problem through the landscape rather than the person – a strategy which more often than not helps to avoid conflict.

3.1 Scarcity

Land is a finite resource. Growing populations and increasing consumption are putting immense pressure on the surface of the planet to provide everything we need to live. We demand more from the world than it can offer – according to research by WWF, our global ecological footprint is an average of 2.2 hectares per person (and rising), but a sustainable level would be 1.8. Where once we mined for fuel fossilized underground – space that could not be cultivated – we are now encouraged to grow it fresh, taking up even more precious room. Offsetting carbon consumption by planting trees takes up more space still. Building new land is one solution to our limited supply (300 islands are being built off the coast of Dubai at Jumeirah, an artificial archipelago for billionaires called 'The World'), but even this is problematic in a world with rising oceans.

Scarcity is accentuated because ownership of land is not distributed evenly.* Look at the numbers:

— If all the cultivated land in the world was distributed evenly between the world's 6.6 billion people, there would be about half an acre per person (about the size of half a football pitch and almost exactly the size of HRH The Prince of Wales's garden at Clarence House in central London).

* President Dwight D. Eisenhower told *Time* magazine in 1961 as he retired to a 200-acre farm near Gettysburg, 'I wanted to take a piece of ground like this that had been sort of worn out through improper use and try to restore it; I just said that when I die I'm going to leave a piece of ground better than I found it.' This is a wonderful sentiment from a peace-loving man, but he of course had the means to buy this land which he had fought to protect as Allied Supreme Commander in the Second World War.

- If we included uncultivated land (but not Antarctica while the ice sheets remain), we would have just over five acres each (the size of the zoo in New York's Central Park).

- Kevin Cahill states in his comprehensive book *Who Owns the World* that just 15% of people own or have a freehold to the 33,558 million acres that make up the world's land above sea level. The rest of us are required by law and convention to have their permission to do anything on it, such as gardening.

- Even in countries where the majority own land, most have very little. So, while 69% of British people have a freehold to land or property, 69% of the kingdom is owned by just 0.3%. A remarkable 89% of Britons are squeezed into dense urban areas, having on average only 0.07 acres of living space each.

- But to hell with *averages*: I would be happy with 0.07 acres (the size of the luxurious suite on the 53rd floor of the Ritz Carlton, Tokyo), when I have 0.01 acres and no garden that I can call my own!

OK, so some people do need more space than others, but the inequality of land rights is totally unjustifiable. In South Africa under apartheid, the black majority were confined to 13% of the land, while the white minority controlled the remaining 87%; even now apartheid has ended, 85% of the country still remains under white ownership. In Brazil, according to figures published by War on Want (WarOnWant.org), just 3% of landowners own two-thirds of all arable land. There are at least twelve million landless people in the country and 80 million hectares of vacant agricultural land (not including the Amazon region). With these two contradictory factors at play, Brazil inevitably records some of the most extensive and successful guerrilla gardening in the world.

Land is not distributed according to need but is used as a financial asset. A landowner can even make money from owning

(*Overleaf*)
A 12,000-strong peasant army storm the 205,090 acres of the Giacometi plantation in Paraná, Brazil.

empty neglected space, just by waiting for it to increase in value,* although most make an income as a landlord of some kind. Their new tenants are in a situation that is far from ideal for gardening. Tenants who garden have to accept that they are doing it for the moment, that it is not a mobile investment and that it is their landlord who will benefit from the value it adds to the property – by tending the garden you could even be pushing your own rent up. Tenants sometimes do not even have permission to garden, in which case you would be a guerrilla gardener in your own back yard! You could just dig up your plants when you move on. Lizzie 002 has lugged fifteen tubs – including a towering bell creeper (*Sollya heterophylla*) – from rented flat to rented flat around southeast England. Christine 1625 called me from her Vauxhall rental to ask me to help her salvage her two hydrangeas (*Hydrangea macrophylla*) rather than hand them on to the new tenants who she knew would neglect them.

The human distribution across the landscape grows more uneven as populations become increasingly urbanized. Since 2006, half the world's people live in cities; three-quarters of us are projected to be urban by 2050. Cities are where jobs are – and where we are allowed to live. Virtually all governments want their cities to become denser, as this is considered to be more efficient, so growth in rural areas is restricted.

Cities are wonderfully vibrant places, but living in a densely populated place comes at the cost of gardening space. Third-world cities are the densest. In 2003, approximately 20% of the developing world's urban population (around 400 million people) lived 'without sufficient space', meaning three or more people were sharing a bedroom.† Cairo has a density of 34,000 people per square kilometre.

---

* These infuriating circumstances would be much reduced if more places introduced a land tax. For more about this, read Henry George's *Progress and Poverty* (1886) or Tony Vickers' *Location Matters* (Shepheard-Walwyn, 2007).
† Eduardo Lopez Moreno and Rasna Warah, 'Urban and Slum Trends', *UN Chronicle*, Vol. XLIII 2, June–August 2006.

Land is so scarce in cities such as this that any form of gardening, even guerrilla gardening, is rare – in Cairo it is guerrilla housing that takes priority: at least 60% live in what is usually called 'unlicensed housing', some of it up to fourteen storeys high.

I live in the most urbanized country and in the largest city in Europe. Although London has a population density of only 4,500 per square kilometre, and almost half the city is open recreational space, access to a garden is not easy. Demand to live here is high, so the prices of houses (and with them their gardens) have climbed to astronomical levels – average house prices in London at the time of writing are more than eight times what they were in 1983. Limited land ownership and planning restrictions have combined to create a land-poor generation, driven into high-density properties like my high-rise apartment, where not even a window box or hanging basket is sanctioned.

A garden is a luxury for anyone here – almost as much as a parking space. Many Londoners who have a front garden have chosen in recent years to pave it over to squeeze in their car.* Even renting an allotment in Britain has become difficult. Thirty years ago, thousands of acres of these rented gardens fell into disuse and were built over by local authorities. Today, however, almost all of Britain's 330,000 allotments are in use.

Scarcity of private garden space is an enemy that drives gardeners to look elsewhere, squeezing greenery on to windowsills and balconies, or to stay indoors and become experts in house plants (my neighbour George has an astonishing collection of cacti and begonias). Or perhaps we should take inspiration from the Frenchman Patrick Blanc and grow *le mur végétal* (the vegetative wall) with plants rooted in felt hung from walls?

* Sir Martin Doughty, chairman of Natural England, stated in July 2007 that in London, front gardens with a combined area 22 times the size of Hyde Park (equivalent to 12 square miles) have been paved over.

Guerrilla gardeners refuse to settle for these alternatives and instead make use of the scraps of land that are available in their neighbourhood. We respond to the population density of cities by increasing the garden density. Through our offensive, we demonstrate that society need not choose between dense cities and garden cities.*

Scarcity of land not only drives people to guerrilla-garden but also threatens the gardens they have created. Guerrilla gardens are tolerated only so long as the owner of the land does not notice, or has no better use for it. That can change. Although the guerrilla gardens that grew in 1970s New York were soon legitimized by New York City authorities, they were by no means secure. Purple 321's Garden of Eden was bulldozed in 1985 to make way for low-income housing, and by the mid-1990s many of the other gardens no longer made economic sense to Mayor Giuliani – a survey of the city's holdings in 1994 concluded that 300 gardens had to go to make way for housing. The gardens were prime real estate, so the fight turned from one against neglect into one against development. The same problem faced the gardeners of the Jardin Solidaire, a popular guerrilla garden in Paris's gritty inner suburb of the twentieth arrondissement, which after five glorious years was closed in 2005 to make way for a gym and underground parking.

In South Central Los Angeles, a magnificent fourteen-acre organic community garden that had been tended for fifteen years by

Purple 321 surveys the Garden of Eden, his incredible 15,000-square-foot creation behind 184 Forsyth Street, New York City, in 1983. Two years later it was destroyed by the city authorities.

---

*The idea of low-density cities with lots of green space was popularized by Ebenezer Howard's influential book of 1902, *Garden Cities of To-morrow*. Howard's model for a sustainable low-density city dominated by public and private gardens was intricately thought through, but often crudely applied by twentieth-century town planners and architects. They were inspired by Howard to move densely populated lower-income communities into high-rise buildings scattered in large communal 'prairies'. Usually publicly owned, these green spaces were too big to be cared for properly, and soon became desolate waste grounds between foreboding towers. The scale, visibility and usually deprived context of these spaces makes guerrilla attacks more difficult, but these huge arenas offer great potential for the guerrilla gardener who steps into the ring.

the African-American and Latino community was bulldozed in 2006. What had once been waste ground earmarked as a site for a new incinerator had instead become a productive haven of Meso-American crops such as pipicha (*Porophyllum tagetoides*), quelite (*Coriandrum sativum*) and rough pigweed (*Amaranthus hybridus*), and 500 young trees, feeding at least 350 people. The garden was created with the city authority in the aftermath of the Rodney King murder, and did much to improve living conditions and morale in the district. But in time the gardeners were caught in a wrangle over land ownership between the city and a developer and, despite strong financial support from Hollywood celebrities and charities, they were refused the land. They turned to guerrilla tactics, holding candle-lit vigils, co-ordinating a 600-strong full-moon bicycle ride chanting 'Save the Farm' and even strapping themselves to the site. In the early hours of 13 June 2006, the Los Angeles County Sheriff's department arrived to evict the gardeners. While most occupants left peacefully, Daryl 1976, an actress, and John 1977 were removed from the walnut tree in which they had been protesting, and some protesters were struck with batons. As the construction of new warehouses began, a couple of protesters made a final futile attempt to stop development by chaining themselves to a bulldozer.

Scarcity is an abstract enemy, even though there is arguably a shortage of land. Accept scarcity as your enemy and it will make targeting someone else's land seem much more sensible. Decide how short of land you are and then take as much as you can garden yourself. But a guerrilla gardener who makes scarcity of gardening space the sole enemy risks striking at locations that are unsuitable as a permanent garden. My recommendation is to focus your attack on neglected land. This is a tangible enemy, and an adversary against which you are more likely to win support.

3.2 Neglect

'Let's fight the filth with forks and flowers' has been my rallying cry at GuerrillaGardening.org. It is the filth – particularly in public space – that is the number one enemy against which most guerrilla gardeners stand united. Visible neglect, be it an abandoned lot piled high with junk, a weedy, litter-strewn roadside verge or a dusty tree pit filled with cigarette butts, is a territorial defeat for everyone.

Waste ground is a waste of space; it is pollution and it is ugly. Neglect proclaims that a community has lost pride and cohesion. When outdoor space is unappealing and even frightening, residents are more likely to stay locked behind closed doors. But when properly cared for, outdoor space becomes living space and a sociable extension of our private domains; whereas neglected space is dead space. Dereliction is an insidious enemy that creeps up unnoticed by those who see the scene regularly. While we are encouraged to take responsibility for our private space, public space is usually the responsibility of a faceless overseer, a distant body that benevolently grants us access to pass through. Yet the space is public, and to me this means it is our responsibility both to care for it and to make good use of it.

Ultimately, public space is neglected because most of us have passed responsibility for it on to someone else. While model citizens may respect the landscape by leaving nothing but footprints and taking nothing but photographs, others litter and vandalize. The products of nature's erosive and creative forces must be tidied up as well. In most societies citizens are not expected to look after public space, beyond throwing litter into bins – it is someone else's job. But so often no one does look after it, whether it is owned by a public or private body. There are all sorts of reasons for this, and we can strengthen ourselves as guerrilla gardeners if we understand them.

UNLOVED LAND

A landowner's priorities may lie elsewhere. If the land is publicly owned, responsibility for it will be one of many items on a list, all competing for time and money. Elections (assuming the land sits in a democratic country) are won on policies that have an obvious impact to us as individuals: employment opportunities, tax, access to education and healthcare, mobility, security and immigration. They are not won on whether the grass has been mown.

There is a lot of unloved land in London, much of it owned by local authorities. Perhaps they have too much to know what to do with it – they certainly put it to poor use. Beyond the official parks and key tourist areas, the landscape as a whole is seen as a blank backdrop, something to debate and invest in only when everything else is taken care of.

This approach is typical of many cities. It is like the way we treat home decorating, as a luxury to indulge in only when the basic needs of food, furniture, warmth and sanitation are taken care of. Just as decorating becomes necessary only after serious damage, perhaps from a flood, so too the upkeep of public space moves up the agenda only if it relates to a more politically charged issue.

Near my home, a shrubby roundabout at the southerly entrance to the Rotherhithe Tunnel under the Thames became headline news after prostitutes were discovered hiding in the bushes. These shrubs were a tangle of unremarkable evergreens, but until the prostitution problem became clear, little horticultural activity occurred on the roundabout. It took becoming a red light district for it to become a greener district.

You might think that it would not take much for an authority to water plants, but it is surprisingly expensive. Phil Hurst, a horticultural contractor to Transport for London, told me that to water the yellow spindle trees (*Euonymus fortunei* 'Emerald 'n' Gold') in the central reservation of the Old Kent Road dual carriageway costs more than £600 each time (this pays for a water tanker, staff time and closing two car lanes to give the gardeners a safety zone) – an amount that would buy 150 new spindle trees at regular garden centre prices – so they are not watered often. Plants are left to nature; the fittest survive and the rest die, left as twiggy sculptures to catch drifting plastic carrier bags on their bare branches.

When I asked a Southwark council estate officer to tell me who did the gardening outside Perronet House (knowing full well it was me) he replied, 'The weather does the gardening.' (In fact, even in the most supportive of climates it still takes a hurricane to prune a shrub.) A Westminster council tree warden described to me how he tried not to plant too many trees, as otherwise people would notice them and they would get vandalized. (Surely the more trees he plants, the more likely it is that some will survive?)

Given the choice of investing in a bright bed of primroses (*Primula* 'Blairside Yellow') or a bright class of pupils we would all choose the latter – but if we took away some of this burden from civic authorities they would not be faced with that choice. Yes, we need them to look after our grand parks and sophisticated recreation spaces, but the pockets scattered around communities, such as roadside verges, planters, tree pits and block parks, can be taken on by us, either as individuals or as a community.

Private owners also neglect and abandon their land, particularly if they live far away from it. As some see it, they need nothing from the space and owe nothing to the community in which it sits – their land is simply an economic asset that they have decided is not worth investing in or selling yet; to the owner the land might as well be precious metal in a bank. But the difference is that the land is not packed away like gold bullion and hidden in a vault, but is a visible blight to everyone. Fortunately the lack of Fort Knox-level security means that the guerrilla gardener can strike.

ORPHANED LAND

More tragic than land that is a low priority are the sites that have become forgotten altogether. Free from any kind of nurture and parenting they are vulnerable to long-term abuse or even kidnapping by private landowners. These are most likely to be pockets of the land like roadside verges and traffic islands – too small to erect a fence around and turn into a park or to sell off and build on, but too big or untidy to be included within the regular street-cleaning itinerary. Justin 734 in San Francisco described the 1,000-square-foot lot he guerrilla-gardened on the corner of Stanyan and Fulton as 'too small for a house but too large to be left the way it was'. It was full of weeds, car parts, garbage, needles and broken glass, but he saw it as a ripe opportunity and stuffed it with plants including fava beans (*Vicia faba*), garlic (*Allium sativum*), Jerusalem artichokes (*Helianthus tuberosus*) and loquat (*Eriobotrya japonica*).

Fringe locations are often lost through being low down on the priority list of a landowner. In the London borough of Hackney, for example, public land without railings, including a lot of roadside verges and flowerbeds, is the responsibility of the Roads, Highways and Pavements Department. Hackney council's website admits that verges are of low importance: 'Grass cutting is actually carried out for highway safety reasons rather than environmental purposes,' it states. Meanwhile, their online maintenance schedule has not only been left blank but includes what looks like an incomplete template: '*The council cuts the grass it owns **enter amount** times throughout summer months.*' Hackney seems to have an orphaned website as well as streets of orphaned land! (Certainly the two guerrilla gardening digs in Hackney that I have participated in were both very revolting patches.) Gardening is to such landowners a tangential activity, a distraction and superfluous cost. Even street cleaners I have met around London see picking litter up from anything other than a paved surface as well beyond their responsibility.

London's transport authority, Transport for London, also has responsibility for some of London's roadside verges, but their expertise in running buses does not extend to fleets of gardeners' wheelbarrows. In New York neglected land tends to fall within the remit of the Housing and Preservation Department, as they are responsible for areas where demolished housing once stood.

Land is also quite often lost through confusion over boundaries and overlapping responsibilities. A traffic island in Westminster Bridge Road that I have guerrilla-gardened is orphaned because it lies in border territory. It is triangular in shape, about 150 square metres in size, and sits in the middle of a busy T-junction barely a mile from the Houses of Parliament. The island is sliced in two by a cycle path, which also marks the boundary between the boroughs of Southwark and Lambeth, so responsibility for the plot is divided. What could have been a front line in civic horticultural one-upmanship, with both councils competitively planting ever more explosive floral displays on their neighbouring beds, instead became an abandoned no-man's-land. Whether deliberately or accidentally, both sides orphaned the two beds in a miserable truce of neglect. Bedraggled cabbage palms (*Cordyline australis*) stood for years in this cratered field, filled with weeds and litter discarded by motorists at the traffic lights, until we transformed it into a huge field of lavender (*Lavandula angustifolia*) and tulips (*Tulipa* 'Isle de France'), free from any interference so far for nearly two years.

Who looks after what is no clearer in the countryside. Freda 850 in High Wycombe, Buckinghamshire, wanted to tidy up the footpath that ran beyond her boundary hedge. It was overgrown with ivy (*Hedera helix*), which was a mess and a threat to Freda's own garden. Freda guerrilla-gardened the patch, cleared most of the ivy and planted some shrubs including laurel (*Laurus nobilis*), cotoneaster (*Cotoneaster horizontalis*) and bluebells (*Hyacinthoides non-scripta*), but when she then enquired of the district council, the Land Registry,

(*Overleaf*) London's guerrilla gardeners have transformed this traffic island in Westminster Bridge Road into an illicit landmark of *Tulipa* 'Isle de France' flowering among *Lavandula angustifolia*.

local solicitors and the highways and byways people, they struggled for several months to identify whose responsibility it was.

Being orphaned is a sad reason for land to be neglected, but it does provide an excellent starting point for the guerrilla gardener. In the case of orphaned spaces we are not so much kidnapping the land as fostering it, and few would have a problem with that. Compared with land that is actively abused by its owners, orphaned land is more likely to be left alone for us to look after. We are taking advantage of the fog shrouding its ownership. It is probable that the improvement made by guerrilla gardeners will be mistakenly attributed by each of the confused landowners to the other, and so ignored.

LITTERED AND WEEDY LAND

Weeds and litter never stop returning to your garden, a shower of neglect that needs to be regularly brushed away. Litter can occasionally be recycled into a garden design but most forms are best harvested and fed to bins. As for weeds, most gardeners define them as 'plants growing in the wrong place' and do what they can to destroy them – they tend to be rampant reproducers that invasively choke space that would otherwise be taken by plants you have cultivated. Whether they are native plants or foreign introductions, weeds are perfectly suited to a fertile environment with no human interference. Weeds are what many guerrilla gardeners clear when first reclaiming a neglected garden space, and they will continue to fight them for the duration of their campaign.

Some troops tell me that weeding is their favourite activity, and for them the pile of uprooted, wilting greenery beside an immaculate brown expanse of fresh naked soil is a sign of victory. But within our ranks are guerrillas who challenge this and embrace the strength of weeds. They argue that we should cherish plants that are so well adapted to otherwise desolate landscapes. If our mission is to create a garden anywhere, then plants that are usually defined as weeds should be included in our arsenal. Look, they say, at the dandelion (*Taraxacum officinale*)* with its beautiful yellow pom-pom flower and delicate globe (or clock) of fine seeds, or the intricate twists of goose grass (*Eleusine indica*) that magically stick to a trouser leg. The sight of a densely packed expanse of dandelions (ticking time bombs poised to be fired across the landscape) could theoretically be either thrilling or terrifying for a gardener.

I know of two guerrilla gardeners who celebrate weeds, and who do not just leave them but positively cherish them. Heather 1986 sees them as refugees in need of a safe haven. She redefines weeds as 'wayward plants' – they are only in the wrong place in the eye of the beholder. Through her website WaywardPlants.org, she finds new homes for all kinds of unwanted plant, whether it is an over-abundant black-eyed Susan (*Rudbeckia hirta*) evicted from a Brooklyn community garden, or a purple loosestrife (*Lythrum salicaria*) that has been torn from a pathway in Cambridge, Massachusetts. Heather told me that she sees 'the value of each individual plant', and endeavours 'to bring out the full potential of their beauty and meaning'.

Helen 1106 could be described as a guerrilla gardening protection force. She has assumed responsibility for weeds in distress by providing them with a shield from pedestrians' trampling. She told me how she noticed a pert dandelion (*Taraxacum officinale*) growing through the concrete bricks on a pavement in the Whitechapel area of London. She was moved by the way it had found a home in such an inhospitable environment, and how it held this precarious position with dignity. Not content with just appreciating the plant, Helen erected a small wooden fence around it as a protective barrier so that others could enjoy it too. Although the fence disappeared

---

* Although dandelions are one of the best-known weeds they have been welcomed in English vegetable gardens since medieval times. Their leaves can be used in salads and their roots roasted and ground to make a coffee-like drink.

soon afterwards, the young dandelion grew to become bigger and stronger and of sufficient sexual maturity to leave a legacy of baby weeds. Helen has documented more of her interventions and creations at StoriesFromSpace.co.uk and describes her activity as 'a quiet revolution'. For those who cherish weeds, the ideal world would be one in which we could leave them alone or, failing that, relocate them to an empty welcoming space and let them get on with life.

Neglected land, even when covered in concrete, will eventually bloom as plants find a foothold in cracks and windswept dirt. The process can create amazing spaces, one of the most celebrated of which is the High Line in New York City. This was an elevated railroad built in the early 1930s for carrying freight, which was then abandoned by 1980. Thirty-three feet above the Lower West Side of Manhattan the remaining 1½ miles of the derelict track turned from a ribbon of concrete, gravel and steel into a wild meadow with patches of woodland. Few had access to the space, but by the late 1990s rumours of the amazing wild oasis in the sky were sufficiently powerful to galvanize locals to save the viaduct from demolition. In 1999 they created 'Friends of the High Line' to advocate its preservation and reuse as a public open space.

The lesson for us comes from what happened next in the High Line story. Preserving the High Line in its wild state was not the intention of most of the activists – this would have been impossible to justify on the densely populated island which is in such need of recreation space, but neither were they going to allow Mayor Giuliani to be triumphant in his plan for demolition. In 2002, with the help of landscape architects, they presented a plan to the city authority for transforming it into a public space. The leading principle of the new park is (according to the designers Field Operations and Diller Scofidio + Renfro) 'to demonstrate the power of nature to take hold in man-made settings' and it takes the form

of a naturalistic spread of plants and weaving paths, in which nature is intricately designed and weeds are tamed. The guerrilla gardener should see weeds in the same way, as inspiration for planning a garden and clues that land is fertile.

WILDERNESS

If weeds are clues of fertile soil and suggest potential for the guerrilla gardener, then a wilderness is blinding confirmation of horticultural opportunity. In short, if a plant in the wrong place is a weed, then many plants in the wrong place are a wilderness. They are mass encampments for the enemy, a danger zone that aggressively fires out strategic missiles to try and reclaim cultivated space. In the whole world there are 19 million square kilometres of land that could be gardened, but only half of it is cultivated; the rest is wild.

Wilderness on the High Line: 1½ miles of derelict elevated railway line along the far west side of Manhattan.

I am aware that some will be appalled by my stance. Whereas fans of weeds are few and far between, there is much less of a consensus about whether 'wilderness' is friend or foe. Most of us have no difficulty in removing handfuls of naturally sown plants growing in our garden, but even with these, when the handfuls become great mounds it can trigger a twinge of discomfort – not because of the effort involved in clearing them but because the scale seems brutal.

Clearing wilderness creates very tangible scenes of destruction. Until a garden grows in its place, the bare earth and piles of torn-up greenery are a violent symbol of a battle with nature; whereas the creativity and productivity of nature left alone is beautiful and reassuring to see – when nature creeps back over land that humans have neglected and polluted it feels as if the world is returning to its virgin state.

But encouraging wilderness is not gardening. To garden is to challenge wilderness – were the landscape left wild there would be no gardens or gardeners. Even when the eighteenth-century landscape architect William Kent 'leaped the fence, and saw that all nature was a garden' (as Horace Walpole put it in his essay 'On Modern Gardening'), he did not sit back and enjoy it. Instead, he smoothed and softened it by scattering and sprinkling naturalistic features when building stately English parks. Guerrilla gardeners can do the same (by which I mean scatter and sprinkle naturalistic features, not build stately English parks – unless you happen to be unusually resourceful).

Although describing the land as 'neglected' suggests that it was once cultivated, and 'wild' implies it has never been touched by humans, *never* is a long time and human impact travels far into supposedly 'wild' places. These areas are not necessarily as natural as they seem (though I shall resist the temptation of debating what 'natural' really means), so see them as neglected land and you will not feel so bad creating a garden there.

Clear-cut boundaries do exist to protect wilderness – around national parks, UNESCO sites and all manner of other special designated areas – but some guerrilla gardeners choose to cross them. For those who decide to do so the landscape offers tempting opportunities. To them, the potential for immediate profit seems much more valuable than the rare creatures and treasury of genetic code the land holds, but ultimately the cost to everyone of gardening in protected wilderness is high. The greatest damage is caused by farmers who illegally fell rainforests. In the Mato Grosso area of Brazil, 540,000 hectares were illegally cleared between 2001 and 2004 to make way for crops, particularly soya beans (*Glycine max*). Increasing soya crops cuts down the price of food, but felling trees reduces carbon dioxide absorption, reduces rainfall and increases global temperature. Even the soya specially adapted to tolerate a tropical climate does not live long in this landscape, and when it dies the land is left exhausted.

Away from the wilds of the South American rainforest, on the genteel English Riviera, Margaret 2878 says she likes nothing more than 'slashing and burning' brambles that grow in the churchyard of St Andrew's, the Greek orthodox church of Torre in Devon. Yet Margaret is a guerrilla gardener better known for the wild garden she has made than for her attacks on wilderness. The story of Margaret points to a middle ground for the guerrilla gardener and our relationship with wild landscapes.

Margaret's guerrilla gardening began as surreptitious clearance of the overgrown churchyard that backed on to her garden. It had become a wilderness after years of neglect – tombstones were obscured by tangles of blackberry (*Rubus fruticosus*), ivy (*Hedera helix*) and bindweed (*Convolvulus arvensis*), and the unruly space had become a no-go zone for all but drunks and drug addicts. Margaret's intervention gradually returned the place to an orderly grass lawn and allowed memorials to be repaired. After a year she went legal and got support from the council.

Her taming of wilderness had brought with it a certain sterility and Margaret wanted to bring life back to the graveyard. One of her troops, Mark 2941, suggested a wildflower meadow. This did not mean leaving an area to return to nature; creating this field of natives required a great deal of gardening. They strimmed the grass down to rough tufty clumps and planted plugs of native Devon flowers in the gaps: primroses (*Primula vulgaris*), cowslips (*Primula veris*), snake's head fritillary (*Fritillaria meleagris*), wild garlic (*Allium ursinum*) and red campion (*Silene dioica*). This kind of wilderness is the most appropriate for the guerrilla gardener – it is a tweaked and tamed wilderness, and gardening it gives us a role as well as a practical, sustainable landscape.

Wild gardening comes with one serious drawback: the very illusion of being wild means that it is not obviously a garden. Even though it is far from neglected, the gentle approach to cultivating the space means that the care it is receiving may not be clear to passers-by or indiscriminate civic mowers. Nine months after it

was established in the churchyard, Margaret's wildflower meadow was attacked by the local council mower. Incredibly, despite Margaret's protests and the council's apology, two months later they made the same mistake and mowed it again. Similar devastation has occurred in west London, where in 2006 Brita 1198 lost a guerrilla-gardened wildflower meadow she and fellow professional landscape architects had sown on the traffic island by the Great West Road.

Guerrilla gardeners who actively create wilderness must accept that it is a creation, and not a real wilderness. If people are to be tricked into thinking it entirely natural, it will need to be protected from those who might attack it as if it were neglected land. A wild garden invites the wilder elements of the public. Where the risk is greater, in more populated areas, a fence is the obvious solution – think of your wild garden as a caged animal, enclosed for its own protection. You could be on your way to creating a nature reserve.

But these security measures are difficult to implement for guerrilla gardeners. Because of the vulnerability of informal wildernesses, the best places for them to be cultivated in urban environments may not be public spaces, but sheltered private gardens. A guerrilla gardener who has a private garden should perhaps create wilderness there, and concentrate on tidying up public space.

3.3 Other Areas

Neglected space is top of the list for the guerrilla gardener, as success is most likely to be achieved here. But scarcity of land also drives guerrilla gardeners to question the use of other terrain that is not so neglected.

LAWNS

Take lawns, for example. On the one hand we like them. An expanse of blank grass is great for knocking a ball around and a good place for a picnic. Grass verges are a neat, water-absorbent frame to tarmac roads. Laid out in front of a house, at the heart of a town or as flowing green ribbons along highways, they remain a sign of civilization – any vision of a perfect community will include a beautiful living carpet of lush turf.

But lawns are also trouble. As a status symbol for seventeenth-century English aristocrats, they were deliberately extravagant, unproductive, animal-free expanses; this indulgence continues. Many so-called lawns do not serve as open space for humans to enjoy, and instead are fenced off. Gardeners who maintain lawns become drivers of energy-guzzling machines (one hour of power-mowing emits pollution equivalent to driving 350 miles by car), dopers with chemicals and irrigators on an industrial scale. There is little creativity required (other than choosing which direction to mow the stripes), and there is nothing to harvest but piles of grass cuttings (which quickly overwhelm a compost heap).

Inevitably the cost and boredom of maintaining lawns means they easily become neglected. In the village of Huétor Vega in southern Spain Michele 014 struck the bald patches of the tatty public lawns with plants such as asparagus fern (*Asparagus densiflorus* 'Sprengeri') that could survive without sprinklers (and nibbling from an occasional stray goat). Heather 1196 advocates digging up lawns altogether and founded FoodNotLawns.com to champion their transformation into productive spaces. She calculates the average American lawn could produce enough vegetables to feed a family of six and even have a small recreational lawn area. During both World Wars the British and Americans made lawns more productive. London's Hyde Park was turned into allotments in 1940 and in the First World War President Woodrow Wilson put sheep on the White House lawns.

(*Previous page*) During the First World War President Woodrow Wilson had sheep graze on the White House lawns to save the manpower needed to mow them. Wool from the sheep was sold to raise funds for the Red Cross.

But lawns are a difficult enemy to conquer. Attacking a neat one will infuriate the landowner much more than if the land was neglected. A plant will be noticed, and even an invisible bulb will be slashed back by the mower when it sprouts. Heather could not risk attacking her lawn in Eugene, Oregon, because her landlord would have evicted her for vandalism, so she became a guerrilla gardener in an unloved grassy corner of a park. Follow her example and concentrate on attacking *neglected* lawns.

ROADS

Even without vehicles, roads take up space, absorb heat, prevent the absorption of rainwater and so create unwelcome heat islands and exacerbate flooding. Add the cars and you introduce exhaust and noise pollution to the environment. There are guerrilla gardeners who see planting as a weapon to be directed towards these great black ribbons that mark our landscape. But picking a road as your enemy is not a straightforward path.

On 13 July 1996, the direct action group Reclaim the Streets decided that a stretch of the M41 motorway in west London would be better if planted with trees – no, not on the verge but right in the fast lane. An army of 3,000 protesters occupied a three-quarter-mile stretch of the road, drilled a hole and planted two small trees. A 25-foot-high carnival figure and loud techno music cleverly disguised a labourer and the sound of his pneumatic drill. While the trees did not last the night, the group's message of making cities greener was picked up by some of the press. But the repairs to the road cost £10,000 – a sum that could have paid for a lot of tree-planting in places where the trees did not obstruct motorways.

A less destructive act of guerrilla gardening against roads, in fact a far more sophisticated and thought-provoking one, occurred in San Francisco on 16 November 2005, and it has since become a highly successful global campaign. John 1013, Matthew 1014,

Blaine 1015 and Gregory 1016 objected to 70% of the city's downtown outdoor public space being used by private vehicles. Their response, carried out under the banner of REBAR, an art collective, was to fill a parking space for a couple of hours with a small park – turf, a hornbeam (*Carpinus caroliniana*), protective railings and an elegant bench – an act they labelled 'PARK(ing)'. They paid the meter (although technically the fee only covered vehicular parking), and vacated the spot when the money ran out, but PARK(ing) challenged the city's designated role for the space. The following year the Mayor gave up his parking space for the day to make way for a PARK(ing) space, and cities around the world have copied the gesture.

Gardens on roads are mostly temporary – the plants that are used here are either short-lived kamikaze martyrs or mobile flower arrangements. They are employed for propaganda purposes. Those who really love to garden, myself included, are not particularly interested in these stunts; we want our gardens to have longer lives. In Toronto, Michael 1954 and his friends have addressed the issue of excessive amounts of space allocated to parking in a less ephemeral way. They filled an old car, appropriately called a Dodge Spirit, with soil and plants, painted it with flowers and parked it (or should I say planted it) outside their restaurant in Augusta Avenue. It is called the Community Vehicular Reclamation Project, and has sat there on and off for two years, providing long-term greenery and a comfortable grassy bonnet.*

COMMERCIAL POLLUTION

Cities are illuminated all year round with colourful advertising hoardings, relentlessly propagating their messages to passers-by, sometimes with a chuckle, sometimes with a genuinely useful piece

---

* Although Michael and his friends received parking tickets and the Dodge Spirit was almost impounded, the city eventually agreed to accept it as public art and have given permission to have the CVRP on the street, free of charge, for six months of the year.

of information, more often than not making a tedious promise of a better life in exchange for your cash. Mark Reddy, one of London's most acclaimed advertising art directors, told me his posters are 'works of art, there to make the world a more beautiful place'. Not everyone agrees. In December 2006 the Mayor of São Paulo, South America's largest and most prosperous city, banned all outdoor advertising, describing it as visual pollution. Elsewhere in the world it is down to activists to attack it.

Adbusters (Adbusters.org), an anti-consumerist organization in Canada, has devised numerous methods of attacking commercial messages. One of these is to grow ivy (*Hedera helix*) up billboards, and in May 2001 they gave away packets of seeds to help readers of their magazine get started (though these seeds would have had little chance to germinate and grow up frequently refreshed billboards). In Rotterdam, Helmut 1831 was irritated by the big new billboards planted all over the city, so he designed a gardening scheme to obscure them. Dressed as municipal workers, he and a friend planted an elm (*Ulmus wallichiana*) in front of a huge Volvo ad on the Dorpsweg. The tree was chosen for its perfect ad-busting credentials – fast growth, neat size and dense crown. Unsurprisingly, it was removed only a few days later.

In Portland, Oregon, Sandy 990 had a slightly longer-lasting ad-busting effect with her guerrilla garden. She subverted the logo of America's oldest Mercedes-Benz dealership by turning their three-pointed star-in-a-circle into the similar fork-shaped peace symbol.* The Mercedes logo was made from an eight-foot-wide box hedge (*Buxus sempervirens* 'Suffruticosa'), so it required only a little guerrilla gardening to make the change. Sandy measured the hedge, bought some box plants to match and struck at 10.30pm on 18 March 2007.

* Designed by Gerald Holtom in 1958 for the Campaign for Nuclear Disarmament, but now used widely by many different peace movements.

For three weeks no one at Mercedes noticed the change in their corporate identity. It took a routine inspection from the dealership's landscape contractor to remove Sandy's bush, but she soon spotted it dumped near by and restored it for another fortnight.

3.4 And Beyond ...

It is perhaps inevitable that areas of neglected space are sometimes improved by guerrilla forces in other ways than gardening. Pavements, fences, roads, benches and phone boxes all require regular care and, if poorly maintained, can look bad and fail to function. Arguably these amenities are more important than public gardens – people can be hurt tripping up on wobbly paving stones or swerving to avoid pot-holes – but laying down tarmac or rewiring a phone box are more challenging than gardening. I see guerrilla gardening as freeing up resources for landowners to concentrate on these more technical problems. But some people have the skill to sort out these problems illicitly with sporadic guerrilla activity.

The Space Hijackers (SpaceHijackers.co.uk), a London group who call themselves 'anarchitects', highlighted their disagreement with a council policy of removing public benches by screwing a new one to a pavement in Bloomsbury, an act they labelled 'guerrilla benching'. In Huddersfield, Yorkshire, a resourceful resident was so fed up with the pot-holed roads that he took direct action. He had no access to fresh tarmac or a steamroller, so he armed himself with the same yellow paint that road maintenance teams use to mark patches needing attention. He walked the streets spraying circles to highlight where he wanted repairs, and soon the press dubbed him the 'Yellow Pimpernel'. The council tracked him down and insisted he turn in his equipment, arguing that gas and water pipes would be punctured if resurfacers followed his instructions.

I myself have done a little late-night guerrilla DIY by helping Tom 354, an investment banker, repaint a rusty old Victorian A-Type pillar-box in Barons Court Road, London.* Our action seemed strangely appropriate since in the Post Office's very own magazine the pillar box was recently described as 'a red revolutionary – the Che Guevara of Acacia Avenue'.

The most astonishing act of clandestine renovation I know of was undertaken in Paris by a group called the Untergunther. The press describe them as a 'cultural guerrilla movement', whose purpose is to restore France's cultural heritage. They targeted the Panthéon, a vast eighteenth-century neo-classical church and burial place for the nation's most celebrated. More specifically it was the clock they set about repairing, which had been left to rust since the 1960s. In September 2005, the group (one of its members is a professional horologist) hid themselves in the building when it was locked for the night and created a secret workshop in a cavity under the dome. It took them a whole year to repair, but finally they revealed their triumphant restoration to the authorities. Prosecution was only narrowly avoided, and the force has since gone underground, vowing to continue their campaign in other areas of the nation. Let us hope that this skilled and dedicated guerrilla movement turn their hands to gardening; the results would surely be superb.

---

* For those who want to paint Royal Mail letter boxes or just recreate the iconic red and black look elsewhere, the official colours can be mixed by most professional paint shops with the following codes: red (Ref 538/BS 381C) and black (Ref 00E53/BS 4800).

A LETTER

TO

The Lord Fairfax,

AND

His Councell of War,

WITH

Divers Questions to the Lawyers, and Ministers:

Proving it an undeniable Equity,

That the common People ought to dig, plow, plant and dwell upon the Commons, without hiring them, or paying Rent to any.

Delivered to the Generall and the chief Officers on Saturday June 9.

By *Jerrard Winstanly*, in the behalf of those who have begun to dig upon *George*-Hill in Surrey.

London: Printed for *Giles Calvert*, at the black Spread-Eagle at the West end of PAULS. 1649.

4. HISTORY

Study the history of guerrilla gardening and you will unearth inspiration. Tempting as it is to think of these tales as the roots of guerrilla gardening, notable blooms from different species would be a more accurate horticultural metaphor. Some seeded and germinated elsewhere, while others rotted and perished.

A pamphlet from 1649 in which Gerrard Winstanley appealed to the government to permit gardening on common land (months after he had started doing so anyway).

St George's Hill, Surrey, England, 1649

Guerrilla gardening occurred long before guerrillas roamed the earth. Precisely when, where and who first cultivated someone else's patch of land without asking them is lost, but I suspect it was not long after

Neolithic people began growing things 14,000 years ago. Later on there is a reference to illicit nocturnal gardening in St Matthew's gospel, but since this is a gloomy parable about sowing weeds in someone else's field I prefer not to dwell on it. Our story therefore begins in seventeenth-century England.

The earliest widely publicized act of guerrilla gardening took place on an English hill in 1649. It was a turbulent time for the whole country. King Charles I had just been beheaded, the Council of State was in charge, and radicals were energetically pamphleting suggestions for the shape of their new society. Among those wanting change was an impoverished textile merchant called Gerrard Winstanley, who was born in Wigan but by this time was living in Surrey. Calling for England's unjust land rights to be corrected, he rallied a group of men and women who became known as the Diggers.

Hungry stomachs caused by record food prices and a lack of land on which to grow their own focused the Diggers' minds on putting the waste ground in their neighbourhood to good use. This was common land, scrubby heath and woodland – such as that which comprised a third of England at the time. Anyone was allowed to walk there, collect wood and berries and graze animals, but no one was allowed to grow anything. This did not make sense to Winstanley. In his pamphlet of 26 March 1649 entitled 'An Appeal to all Englishmen to Judge between Bondage and Freedom' he wrote:

> *The common Land hath laid unmanured all the days of his Kingly and Lordly power over you, by reason whereof both you and your fathers (many of you) have been burdened with poverty. And that land which would have been fruitful with corn, hath brought forth nothing but heath, moss, turfs ...*

A week later, on 1 April 1649, he was guerrilla gardening on St George's Hill, near Weybridge in Surrey. Heath was burned to clear a patch for planting, and parsnips (*Pastinaca sativa*), carrots (*Daucus carota*), beans (*Phaseolus vulgaris*) and barley (*Hordeum vulgare*) were sown. Up to 30 men at once dug during the day.

Winstanley was not at all secretive about his action, inviting passers-by to come and help, promising them meat, drink and clothes, and he spoke ambitiously of thousands joining him over subsequent weeks. His message was that no one should have more land than they could labour themselves, and that labour should be shared, not hired. In his most focused pamphlet, 'The True Levellers Standard Advanced', he stated his reasons:

> *That we may work in righteousness, and lay the Foundation of making the Earth a Common Treasury for All, both Rich and Poor, That every one that is born in the land, may be fed by the Earth his Mother that brought him forth, according to the Reason that rules in the Creation.*

News of what was going on reached the Council of State in London, and it was reported that 'a disorderly and tumultuous sort of people are assembling themselves together at a place called St George's Hill'. They were concerned that this 'ridiculous' activity might grow and become a 'disturbance of the peace and quiet of the Commonwealth',* and so sent a soldier to inspect the activity. The Diggers were duly asked to explain themselves to Sir Thomas Fairfax, Lord General of the Commonwealth, but they had no difficulty in persuading him of their reasonable objectives and peaceful, commonsense approach. Fairfax observed after visiting

---

* Quoted in Lewis H. Berens, *The Digger Movement in the Days of the Commonwealth* (Simpkin, Marshall, Hamilton, Kent, & Co. Ltd, 1906). This book is available free in its entirety online at gutenberg.org/files/17480/17480-h/17480-h.htm.

them 'that they carry themselves civilly and fairly in the country, and have the report of sober, honest men'.* He saw the activity as a local squabble, which presented no threat to national government, and left it to the local authorities to keep order. Unfortunately, then as today, local authorities could not be relied upon to manage such a situation very well.

As other Digger colonies sprung up and Winstanley published more rousing pamphlets, the lords of the manors responded with increasing aggression. The Diggers on St George's Hill were chased into Walton church and imprisoned there, their crop was dug over, and they had their spades stolen and their carts smashed. (One brutal confrontation was reportedly from a group of men dressed as women.) Winstanley was tried at court for trespassing on common land and each Digger was fined the sizeable sum of £10.

In the autumn of 1649, the Diggers moved on to a new plot at Little Heath, near Cobham, where the lord of the manor was sympathetic to their cause. But within weeks the local priest had turned against them, and by spring 1650 their gardening and their resolve had been crushed. Winstanley published one more book in 1652, called *The Law of Freedom in a Platform*. It was an elaborate account of his vision of a utopian society, but England's self-styled Lord Protector Oliver Cromwell ignored Winstanley, who then it seems resigned himself to a quiet life and became a church warden.†

---

* As reported later in a news sheet entitled 'The Speeches of Lord General Fairfax and the Officers of the Army to the Diggers at St George's Hill in Surrey', dated 31 May 1649.
† Today St George's Hill is a heavily fortified luxury residential enclosure, land costs £3 million per acre and it has been home at one time or another to celebrities including Ringo Starr and Tom Jones. Cameras, gates and warnings mark every entry point. On my second visit to investigate I managed to slip in under the electric gate and explore. Past the wooded zone at the base of the hill is an immaculate golf course. Beyond this buffer zone are the residents, hidden away in giant villas behind another layer of thick foliage and high gates. The place could hardly be further away from Winstanley's vision of a shared productive landscape.

Pennsylvania and Ohio, USA, 1801

In early nineteenth-century North America, a guerrilla gardener emerged who was not motivated by a desire to make the world a more beautiful place; nor was he correcting the injustices of society. He was a particularly shrewd businessman.

John Chapman was born in September 1774 into a poor family in Leominster, Massachusetts, in an atmosphere of impending war. He was later apprenticed to an orchard keeper, growing up to make fruit-growing his trade. As a young man he saw there was a business opportunity to be had from moving in advance of settlers heading out west and selling them young apple trees (*Malus domestica*) when they arrived. So, with a sack of apple seeds on his back, he set off to north-western Pennsylvania to start guerrilla gardening.

He could have gardened legitimately – the Holland Land Company was offering tracts for sale to settlers – but Chapman did not bother with this formality. Most landowners lived far away on the east coast and were interested not in cultivating the soil themselves, just in profiting from it. The land he was to attack was neither neglected nor wild; it was the home and hunting ground of Native Americans. So through his guerrilla activity he was potentially making two types of human enemy – and while he did not fear the property magnates on the eastern seaboard, the natives were not so far away.

Chapman avoided confrontation with the local inhabitants by befriending them, speaking their languages and teaching them how to cultivate trees and mix herbal medicines. He cut informal clearings in the abundant landscape and seeded apple trees all around the outskirts of nascent settler towns such as Warren and Franklin in Pennsylvania and Mariette and Mansfield in Ohio. He favoured discreet riverside spots, as it was in these fertile and accessible lands that the settlers were most likely to come and put

down roots. In every inviting patch he planted some seeds, fencing the area to keep away peckish cattle and deer. His guerrilla orchards soon produced seedlings that he sold on to the local inhabitants.

It was a good business to be in – apple trees were an important part of the household for rural settlers, bearing not just fresh fruit but the ingredients for apple butter and cider. The Ohio Land Company even specified that customers had to plant 50 apple trees during their first year of settlement to gain the title to the property.

Chapman kept moving on to stay ahead of the new settlers, and on his travels he would sometimes trade apple trees for food and shelter. As his business grew, he could no longer just plant apple trees informally, so he began to buy and lease land, eventually owning or leasing over 1,500 acres. Records show that he had 15,000 seedlings on a single 42-acre plot in Indiana, so you can imagine how many thousands of seedlings he planted in his life, many of them as a guerrilla gardener.

Berkeley, California, USA, 1969

In the spring of 1969, preparations were being made for the decade's great flowering of counterculture spirit: the Woodstock music festival in upstate New York. Meanwhile, on the other side of the USA, students at the University of California, Berkeley, were planning another great flowering, the transformation of an eyesore on their campus into a park. This was the first grand moment of modern-day guerrilla gardening – though it had yet to be given that name.

The location was a three-acre plot nestled between Dwight Way and Haste. The university had bought it two years before, but building plans had stalled and it sat as a muddy rubble-strewn temporary parking lot. The students had other plans. On 18 April 1969, an announcement in *The Berkeley Barb* from the mysterious

The 1969 Memorial Day demonstration to save the People's Park at which guerrilla gardeners handed out bundles of *Chrysanthemum leucanthemum.*

'Robin Hood's Park Commissioner' (in fact a well-known local man called Stew Albert, recruited by the students), rallied people to gather there and build a 'Power To The People's Park'. This would be a place for free speech but also free love.* Two days later more than 100 people turned up equipped for battle and a party. It all seemed to come together with very little organization. Thousands more, young and old, students and residents, joined them over the subsequent weeks, gardening during the daytime and talking politics at night.

But as the park took shape and became a popular hangout, the university became concerned that their plans for building there were in jeopardy. While they held meetings to try to agree a solution, bigger authorities were preparing to step into the fray. News of the People's Park had reached the mansion of the Governor of California, Ronald Reagan, who took serious objection to the guerrilla gardeners' frontier spirit. He labelled them 'communist sympathizers' and 'sexual deviants' and made plans to eject them.

In the twilight hours of 15 May one hundred California Highway Patrolmen and armed police arrived to close the park. They surrounded it with an eight-foot-high chainlink fence hung with 'No Trespassing' signs. That morning the *San Francisco Chronicle* quoted Reagan as saying, 'If there has to be a bloodbath, then let's get it over with.' News hit the campus. A crowd of 3,000 were already gathered in Sproul Plaza for a rally about the Arab–Israeli conflict, but their protest changed focus. Dan 110, a student leader, took the stage and cried, 'Let's take back the park.' The police shut down the PA system and the protesters rose up and marched down Telegraph Avenue chanting, 'We want the park.' It became what is now known as Bloody Thursday. The angry mass turned a

---

* Decades later Wendy Schlesinger, one of the park's founders, told the press that the park was created primarily as a place for her to continue an illicit tryst, and that the politics came later.

fire hydrant against the police and threw bottles and rocks. Tear gas was hurled back by the authorities and moments later a police car was overturned and burst into flames. Shots were fired and James Rector, a bystander watching from a rooftop, was killed, another man was blinded and more than a hundred were injured. Reagan declared an official state of emergency and summoned the National Guard.

With a cloud of violence over the project the guerrilla gardeners changed tactics and planned a more peaceful demonstration to coincide with Memorial Day, a national holiday to commemorate Americans killed in military conflict. They bought bundles of daisies (*Chrysanthemum leucanthemum*) with $3,000 donated by two elderly Quaker sisters, and when the National Guard rolled in with bayoneted rifles and tear gas the 30,000 demonstrators responded by handing them flowers. A plane flew by hung with a banner declaring, 'Let a thousand parks bloom'. No injuries were reported and photographs of peaceful bouquet-bearing protesters with the National Guard were published in newspapers.

Against a backdrop of war in Vietnam, this peaceful battle at home was particularly poignant and successful. The National Guard retreated, and while the university continued to fight to reclaim the land and skirmishes continued, by September 1972 Berkeley city council had agreed to lease the People's Park site from the university and was encouraging local people to improve the space. Confrontations have periodically flared up since then: in 1991 the university built sand volleyball courts that triggered a riot, and in October 2005 some park supporters began rebuilding the ruined free-cycling 'free box' without permission and were threatened with arrest. The university still owns the land and reluctantly allows the park to remain. The grassy area, shrubberies, children's playgrounds and dog park are appreciated, but have an air of neglect about them, and the debate rumbles on as to how the space should be used.

Bowery-Houston, New York, USA, 1973

The term 'guerrilla gardening' was invented in 1973 by Liz Christy, a young oil painter living and working in New York. Liz noticed tomato plants growing in the mounds of trash that littered derelict lots in her neighbourhood of Bowery-Houston. The plants had clearly sprouted from fruit in the discarded rubbish, and their germination promised potential in the landscape. Likewise local children were finding places to play in the urban wastelands. Taking inspiration from what they saw, Liz and her friends scattered their own seeds in vacant lots and planted empty tree pits. As this small venture flourished, so their ambition grew to make a bigger impact on the neighbourhood: they decided to create a community garden. Recalling the New York of the seventeenth century, in which every house had a garden and pasture for livestock, they wanted a garden that would be a small green oasis in a district of densely built, high-rise gridiron.

In the mid-1970s, inner-city neighbourhoods such as the Lower East Side, Harlem, parts of the Bronx and Brooklyn were decaying, as buildings were neglected, burned and eventually demolished, and New York was collectively at a loss as to how to turn around the decline. The Big Apple (*Malus domestica* 'Red Delicious') was rotten, infested with criminals and afflicted by great swathes of revolting no-go areas. People were fleeing Manhattan to the suburbs of New Jersey, and land in the East Village was worth very little. The impact of dilapidation and disinvestment in New York was so bad that tax revenues declined and the city could no longer even afford to maintain its best public space. Central Park, once the jewel in the crown of Manhattan's parks, was now a place where even the squirrels were allegedly addicted to crack cocaine.

On the northeast corner of Bowery and Houston Streets the guerrilla gardeners found a vacant lot, 300 feet by 50 feet, littered with

twentieth-century urban bric-a-brac. Donald 277, a college student who guerrilla-gardened with Liz in the early days, showed me round the garden on a sunny September morning. He described how it took a year to prepare the ground. Out went the old fridges, bed frames, burnt-out cars and rubble, and in came fresh topsoil, plants, donations from nurseries and horse manure begged from the local police station. This began quite illicitly. The land was publicly accessible, but ownership was lost somewhere between the absentee landowner and New York City, who had the power to repossess land if sanitation taxes were not paid. Liz called her band of friends the Green Guerillas (they briefly toyed with being the Radical Rhizomes).

The *New York Daily News* picked up on their story and reported it as a revolutionary ray of hope. Soon Liz and her troops were in demand across the city, helping others start community gardens in their area. In new territories they sometimes began their attacks by replicating the pioneering spirit of the little tomato plants. Seed bombs were thrown on to the rubble, where they would eventually explode into colour and begin to show the potential for the landscape to be beautified.

The guerrillas gained legitimization after about fifteen months of activity; the city took responsibility for the land ownership and leased it to them for one dollar a year with a very insecure contract. In 1990 the gardeners received greater security by being taken under the wing of the local development group, the Cooper Square Committee. When the neighbouring building was redeveloped they secured protection and even compensation for the disturbance. Thirty-five years on the garden is now a varied scheme including a grove of weeping birch (*Betula pendula*), flowering perennials, vegetables and a grape arbour. A family of turtles swims in a large pool, and the hive is full of bees.

Liz died aged 39, and the garden she began has been named after her (LizChristyGarden.org). Thirty gardeners now regularly look after the plot, and since 2005 the city has recognized it as an official community garden with the same protection as Central Park. The Green Guerillas (GreenGuerillas.org) live on today as a not-for-profit body supporting thousands of community gardeners across New York with plant materials, design assistance, community facilitation and organization.*

Tacamiche, Honduras, 1995

Gerrard Winstanley's seventeenth-century struggle continues today. Powerful owners neglect huge swathes of potentially rich agricultural land, while nearby poor people go hungry; seizing land and growing food on it without permission occurs around the world. The most inspiring recent example is the story of the Tacamiches' battles in Honduras – the original 'banana republic'.

The conflict began to brew when the agricultural labourers on the San Juan banana plantation at Tacamiche went on strike over pay, which was lagging behind the country's high inflation. Their American bosses, Chiquita Brands International, responded by closing down 1,200 hectares of plantation and firing 1,200 workers. Those still employed grudgingly settled the strike and Chiquita set about preparing to sell the old plantation to local producers from whom they could buy bananas (*Musa cavendishii*) more cheaply than when they employed their own unionized labourers.

But the transfer of the land to the local producers was not so simple. In Honduras it is typical for labourers to live and work in the plantations in fully functioning village communities with churches,

---

* Their importance in the city was recognized by Hollywood with the 1990 romantic comedy *Green Card*, in which Andie McDowell plays a Green Guerilla called Brontë. Eight minutes into the film she is seen with her troops at a spectacular dig at a neglected lot in the East Village. A burnt-out car is cleared away, a lorry-load of topsoil arrives, and new raised beds are laid out and planted late into the night.

health centres and tied plots of land on which to grow their own crops. The village at Tacamiche had been built in the 1930s by the plantation. Now out of work and soon to lose their homes, the former labourers were compelled to survive by becoming guerrilla gardeners.

One of them, Jorge Antonio, described to the *New York Times* how Chiquita had sucked the juice from the plantation and abandoned it without a thought for the fate of those who lived there. Antonio and his fellow ex-workers used 250 hectares of the abandoned plantation to plant maize (*Zea mays*) and beans (*Phaseolus vulgaris*). They had reason to be optimistic about their stance because in 1983, when their employer had fired 3,000 workers from its Costa Rica plantation, a similar land occupation and guerrilla gardening had soon led to the Costa Rican government promising them land.

A decade on, the response was different. On 26 July 1995 Chiquita sent in 400 policemen and soldiers wielding baseball bats and firing tear gas and rubber bullets to evict their former employees. Eighty hectares of corn and beans were destroyed and 26 plantation residents were arrested. But the guerrilla gardeners stood their ground. They lobbed rocks and beat back the police. With their eviction date postponed and cheered by a national outcry in their support, they used the lull in battle to expand their land holding by another 50 hectares and offered to buy the land.

But there was no deal. The combined corporate and government forces planned another unpopular eviction attack once they were sure there would be no slip-ups. They got presidential approval and on 1 February 1996, with an army of 500 government troops, a 400-strong mob of Chiquita workers, a 'field judge' and tear gas, they stormed the plantation. One hundred Tacamiches were arrested. The hired men bulldozed crops, homes and even the community's churches. One of the the victims, Wilfredo Cabrera, told the *New York Times*, 'It was very painful to see all of our corn, peppers, tomatoes, carrots, and melons being ploughed over by bulldozers.'

According to local and international human rights groups, Chiquita's closure of the plantation to resolve the strike and eviction of the Tacamiches were in breach of Honduran land reform law as well as the United Nations International Covenant on Economic, Social and Cultural Rights. After the eviction the Honduran government and Chiquita did some half-hearted rebuilding by way of compensation, but the Tacamiches held out for more, and so effective was their campaign that eighteen months later they were given decent new homes, churches, a fish farm and land to garden.

The high-profile struggle of these guerrilla gardeners marked a turning-point in Chiquita's attitudes to their labour force in Honduras. In 2001 the company signed a landmark agreement with their long-time antagonists – the International Union of Food Workers and the Latin American banana workers' union group (COLSIBA) – to respect the International Labour Organization conventions.

Westminster, London, England, 2000

On 1 May 2000, on the large grassy traffic island directly outside the Houses of Parliament, guerrilla gardening hit the headlines on English soil. Or at least that is what the agitators called it. As we shall see, this famous act of so-called guerrilla gardening was actually something rather different.

Although May Day is traditionally a time to celebrate the arrival of summer and the natural fertility of the season, since the late nineteenth century it has also been a day marking the struggles of the labouring classes and their fight against exploitation. By the turn of the twenty-first century the day had evolved into an occasion to attack capitalism, capitalists and all those who permitted their existence. The theme changed slightly from year to year, depending on which part of the loosely organized anti-capitalist coalition shouted loudest, and serious messages easily got lost or distorted.

In 2000, an eco-warrior contingent brought the marginal movement of guerrilla gardening to the fore by using it as a symbolic act. The leaders were the direct action network Reclaim the Streets who campaign for 'global and local social-ecological revolution(s) to transcend hierarchical and authoritarian society'. They organized a mass bike ride from Hyde Park and together with a samba band headed for Parliament Square, where 10,000 protesters had gathered. Their banners proclaimed 'Resistance is Fertile' and 'Let London Sprout'. The turf at the centre of the square was dug up and laid across the main road around it, and in its place an assortment of herbs, apple trees (*Malus domestica*) and runner beans (*Phaseolus coccineus*) were planted, and hemp seeds (*Cannabis sativa*) were scattered. The planting was enriched with exotic lion dung, there was a small pond, and 'additional decoration was provided by gnomes and potted primroses' (*Primula polyanthus*). James Matthews, a British soldier who had served in Bosnia, climbed up the bronze statue of Winston Churchill in Parliament Square, daubed it with the hammer and sickle and decorated the old man's bald head with a strip of turf (predominantly *Lolium perenne*) in the style of a punkish Mohican haircut.

The photo of Churchill as an eco-punk* and a headline screaming about guerrilla gardening made entertaining press but did little for guerrilla gardening as a movement. While the streets were reclaimed from cars for an afternoon of fun, the protesters left a muddy mess that was not nearly as fertile as their witty banners had claimed – turf is difficult to grow at the best of times and was never going to thrive on Churchill's barren forehead.

* The graffiti artist Banksy has now immortalized the image in one of his stencil paintings.

Deployed this way, the plants were weapons with no long-term positive impact. They became little more than a low-carbon, easy-to-clean alternative to spray paint and petrol bombs. Gardeners were unsympathetic. The establishment was furious and Matthews was fined £250 for his part in the action.

The long-term impact of the event was to deter more moderate elements in society from associating themselves with 'guerrilla gardening' – curious and tentative guerrilla gardeners still anxiously ask me about it. Until recently it was the biggest publicity that guerrilla gardening had ever received. While I am happy to accept all sorts of different forms of guerrilla gardening in the ranks, this particular stunt, so close to my home, still irritates me. I wish it had been tagged with some other name than guerrilla gardening, because while there was a guerrilla spirit about it, there was not much of a gardener's love. I call it 'renewable graffiti', whereas genuine guerrilla gardening is 'living graffiti'.

Elephant & Castle, London, England, 2004

My first guerrilla garden by the entrance of Perronet House, London.

I was completely unaware of any of the history described above, or even of the existence of the term 'guerrilla gardening' when, one Tuesday night in October 2004, I began illicitly cultivating the neglected public planters at the base of my ten-storey 1970s tower block in Elephant & Castle. The split-level flowerbeds beneath Perronet House were a grim tangle of old shrubs, builder's debris and litter. Even weeds seemed unwelcome in the barren bed next to the tower's front door. Happiest were an old white butterfly bush (*Buddleia davidii*), rampant ivy (*Hedera helix*) and periwinkle (*Vinca minor*), but this axis of evil had thuggishly taken over what the architect had presumably imagined as splendid interlocking beds cascading down from the first-floor entrance to the parade of busy bus stops below.

By the time I began guerrilla gardening I had been renting a flat in Perronet House for five months, at a time of year when a gardener should have been busy on the beds, but all I noticed was flourishing litter. Rather than wait for the council to sort them out I decided to do so myself.

My need to garden was something I had overlooked when choosing to live in a tower block. I had failed to realize how much I enjoyed gardening and how much I would miss it. Now it came to me that my need to garden could be satisfied through the great potential offered by the public beds. Discreetly gardening there seemed like the most straightforward way of dealing with both the filth around me and the frustration of not having a garden. At this time I had no intention of cultivating other neglected land or encouraging others to join in.

So I found myself there at two o'clock in the morning, my body charged with tea, pulling out weeds, digging in manure and planting red cyclamen (*Cyclamen persicum*), lavender (*Lavandula angustifolia*) and three spiky cabbage palms (*Cordyline australis*). I felt like some kind of mischievous tooth fairy or green-fingered vandal. I hoped that by gardening at such a strange hour I would avoid trouble with neighbours and with the council, both of whom, I feared, would be irritated by a meddling newcomer. That first evening I improved the patch by the main entrance, but there was a lot more gardening to be done and the plants had years of growth ahead of them.

The plants survived the next few uncertain days and I picked up a little gossip that the improvement had been noticed by residents – most assumed that the council had finally got round to doing something. I was not yet confident enough to out myself to my neighbours. I preferred to remain undercover and continue my gardening uninterrupted.

Yet it was all too much fun to keep totally secret. I was happily entertaining friends with my exploits, and I chose to spread the word further by blogging it, including a photographic diary of the transformation. I was intrigued to see who would find the website and what they would make of it. Another advantage of the blog was that I could easily direct sympathetic people to a record of the garden's development. I assumed that those who found it through search engines would mostly be supportive. I did not give thought to the name of the blog when I registered the domain name. GuerrillaGardening.org seemed to sum it up, and for several weeks I even thought I had invented the term. Weeks later, when scanning how my site was performing in search engines, I was amazed to discover all sorts of other references to guerrilla gardening. It was a brilliant moment. There were guerrillas all over the place, pages of websites, the original Green Guerillas, ecological action groups, news stories about the 2000 May Day protests and so on. I realized that I was part of something much bigger.

As the flowers flourished and I became more confident that Southwark council was uninterested in what I was doing, I began to tend the gardens at more sociable hours. In time my blog attracted interest, and it has grown from being a record of what I am up to into a loose organization for other guerrilla gardeners too. Visitors sign up as troops, long-time guerrilla gardeners surface on the community forum, sharing their experiences and sending links to their own websites, and newcomers post messages offering their support, looking for advice and announcing digs.

As for my guerrilla gardening outside Perronet House and beyond . . . well, the battles continue. Year one's trouble-free gardening did not last. The story of what happened next will be continued in Part Two.

PART TWO:
THE MANUAL

5. THE ARSENAL

A guerrilla gardener really needs little more than a packet of seeds or some bulbs to strike out and join the front line. There is no need for massive armament. While an enthusiastic gardener can easily acquire a tool for almost every job, an outfit for any climatic condition and a precious collection of ornamental plants, a guerrilla gardener's arsenal is, by necessity, more streamlined. It is unlikely you will have a tool shed in which to stockpile your resources,* and your plants will not have the security they would on your own land. When choosing what to stash and carry into the field, be efficient, adaptable and resourceful.

Seed bombs moulded in the shape of 9mm pistols by Christopher 1594 in Richmond, Virginia.

---

* Having said that, the once guerrilla, now legitimate, Clinton Community Garden in New York City has a huge double tool shed.

5.1 Plants

At the heart of our arsenal plants replace bombs and bullets. More sophisticated than the most devastating WMD, these weapons are programmed with DNA that will explode into life in the right conditions. There is always a plant tailored to the conditions of your battlefield. Choose your weapon well and it will grow and flourish, even propagating itself further afield.

Before choosing what to grow you need to ask yourself questions about your mission. What has motivated the fight? Is your priority beautification or harvest? Are you encouraging native species, or is your vision an incongruous horticultural statement? What constraints do you face in this warfare – from the landscape, from enemies? Are you starting with a particular location in mind and finding plants to suit it, or is it the other way round? Do you want to become a regular troop or just make occasional sorties? How will you ensure the community benefits from your gardening, and is this important to you? The more public your space, and the less frequently you are able to care for it, the less like regular gardening your mission becomes and the more specialized your choice of plants needs to be.

Using horticultural weapons in public space requires careful consideration. While private gardeners can explode anything in their back garden – like US weapons testers in the Nevada desert – guerrilla gardeners are at the front line from the start. Drawing on the experience of guerrilla gardeners from around the world, I will offer some guiding principles and suggest some hero plants that will best enable you to realize your ambitions. This is not an encyclopaedic catalogue, more a short list with a bias towards plants suited to the cooler northern latitudes, since that is where the guerrillas I have encountered have most experience. Pick and choose from them and mix approaches that best suit your war zone.

I have highlighted particularly suitable plant species and cultivars within each genus, but it is likely that many others will also flourish. Share what works for you. I encourage readers to pool their horticultural knowledge within a local community forum at GuerrillaGardening.org.

IMPACTFUL PLANTING

A guerrilla gardener should consider applying elements of 'shock and awe' to planting. Make your garden stand out from the context in which it sits. Wow the public into appreciating it. Eye-catching plants will make it obvious an attack has occurred. Consider how most passers-by will see the garden. Plant bigger and bolder the faster traffic passes by so your efforts are noticed. Using a mature flowering plant will create a big impact immediately and so help ensure your planting is not overlooked or mistaken as a weed. However, budgets and logistics may require guerrillas to use seeds and wait patiently for the strike to show a positive result. A high-impact planting scheme is also more vulnerable to theft by trophy hunters, so consider this approach with caution.

There are three key horticultural tactics you can deploy to achieve maximum impact:

Colourful plants Bright plants, whether with vivid blooms or showy leaves, are a priority when applying the impact strategy. Plant en masse, so that large blocks of colour are visible from a distance:

— **Daffodils** (*Narcissus* e.g. 'Jetfire', 'Vulcan') and **tulips** (*Tulipa* e.g. 'Emperor', 'Kingsblood') should be planted in autumn. By springtime they will have become a legion of bright trumpets marching 15cm (6in) high, and they will return year after year.
— **Canna lilies** (*Canna* e.g. 'Tropicana', 'Bengal Tiger') have brightly coloured flowers and striking paddle-shaped tropical-

looking leaves. The canna is a herbaceous perennial and is available with flowers in all sorts of shades of red, pink, yellow and orange. It is also known as 'Indian Shot' because its tiny hard seeds make good bullets.

Helianthus annuus towering boldly over a traffic island in Blackfriars Road, central London.

— Primroses (*Primula* e.g. 'Wanda Supreme Series') are herbaceous perennials that form neat spots of colour, with bell-shaped flowers of assorted blinding colours that pop up from a base of ground-hugging broad leaves. They flower from winter to mid-spring. A huge variety of primroses are available beyond the common vigorous one recommended here.

Incongruous plants You can make your mark on the landscape by planting something utterly out of place. Big or peculiar-looking flowers and trees are the most impactful way of doing this:

— Sunflowers (*Helianthus annuus*) radiate their yellow sunshine from stalks up to 5m (16ft) high. Although they prefer moist ground, you can grow them up to about 2m (7ft) high in dry soil (and you can eat the seeds). They help break up compacted soil and also extract lead from the ground (but avoid eating the flowers if you are using them to clean land in this way).

— Christmas trees (*Picea abies*) are common additions to urban centres for a couple of months, but only as depressing dying specimens decked out in a plastic and electric garb that ostensibly celebrates a famous birth but is actually marking the plant's funeral. Grow one that the community can enjoy throughout the year. If you have room, go for a 40m (130ft) beauty. Otherwise try a dwarf cultivar such as 'Gregoryana'.

— Coastal redwood (*Sequoia sempervirens*) or giant redwood (*Sequoiadendron giganteum*) are the tallest trees in the world. Although naturally only found in western USA they can thrive in other places too if summers are cool and damp. They are tolerant of winds and pollution and can live for thousands of years. Unfortunately they will only tower over bug life while we are alive, but why let time hold you back from aiming high?

Fragrant plants Where pedestrians and cyclists abound, pungent plants will be appreciated. In polluted cities they provide a natural air-freshener. I love the smell of guerrilla gardens in the morning.

— **Lavender** (*Lavandula angustifolia*) has fragrant leaves all year round and sweet-smelling flowers during the summer. It is also tolerant of fairly poor, dry soil and attracts bumblebees.
— **Common sage** (*Salvia officinalis*) is an evergreen perennial that bears fragrant hairy leaves of up to 8cm (3in) long all year round. Available in a variety of flower colours, and edible too, it enjoys full sunshine.
— **Mock orange** (*Philadelphus coronarius*) is a deciduous shrub, 3m (10ft) tall with very fragrant white cup-shaped flowers in early summer. It is native on scrubland and rocky hillsides around the world, so will survive in a fairly poor, previously neglected environment, and it loves alkaline soil.

RESISTANT PLANTING

To ensure your resistance to neglect is fertile rather than futile, your plants must be resistant too. They will need to cope with harsher environmental conditions than those in a sheltered domestic garden. Your battleground may be quite hostile to nature, so unless you are to be on constant mercy missions you will need to plant species that can tough it out. The target you have in mind may be neglected because it has proved difficult to cultivate in the past; perhaps it is chronically short of the essential ingredients for plant life – water, light and nutrients. Familiarize yourself with the plot, and learn from what is there already. You may be able to remedy some of the conditions that limit your choice of plants, but try to work with nature and choose plants that are already tailored to the situation.

Drought-tolerant plants If regular rain or watering is unlikely, use plants that will acclimatize to the prevailing conditions. Mediterranean and alpine plants are happy in dry, temperate climates. Something with small or oily leaves is most likely to survive through periods of drought:

— **Stonecrop** (*Sedum acre*) is a drought-tolerant perennial succulent that grows almost anywhere, appreciating but not requiring full sunshine, and surviving in poor soil. It is available in many different flower colours and evergreen varieties.
— **Baby's breath** (*Gypsophila paniculata*) is an alpine plant, happy on dry, stony hillsides, that grows as a low mound up to 45cm (18in) wide and is dotted with tiny white five-petalled flowers. It can tolerate short droughts.
— **Candytuft** (*Iberis sempervirens*) also grows in mounds so makes good ground cover. While some candytufts are annuals, *I. sempervirens* is evergreen, lasts more than a year and bears abundant white flowers in late spring and early summer. Candytufts attract hoverflies, a useful ancillary force against garden pests.
— **Hebe** (*Hebe* x *franciscanailla*) is an evergreen shrub that tolerates pollution, fairly dry soil, salty environments and even shade. It bears pink-tinged purple flowers from summer to autumn.

Shade-tolerant plants Most plants require four to eight hours or more of sunshine a day, so if your patch is perpetually shaded by a tall building or mature trees you will need plants that are adapted to these conditions:

— **Common foxglove** (*Digitalis purpurea*) is an imposing woodland plant that will grow in almost any soil and situation. Its lance-shaped flower-heads laden with purple, pink or white bells tower up to 2m (7ft) in a season, and it easily self-seeds ready to return the next year in great abundance. If you grow it from seed it will flower in the second year.

— **Siberian squill** (*Scilla siberica*) is a bright blue, bulbous perennial with dazzling nodding flowers on bending stalks 15cm (6in) long that will rampage across shady ground beneath trees and beyond, flowering in springtime.

— **Cyclamen** (*Cyclamen hederifolium*) loves dry shade and provides autumn and winter colour with its pink flowers. The plant dies back entirely in summer but will return the next year.

Poor soil-tolerant plants If your sick barren soil cannot easily be remedied, choose plants that are happy rooted in ground that is low in nutrients:

— **Nasturtiums** (*Tropaeolum majus*) run rampant in poor soils, spilling their red, orange and yellow trumpety flowers and kidney-shaped leaves in trails across the ground or up a fence. The flowers last all summer. They die back but leave seeds, so even more plants will grow back the next year. The leaves and flowers can be used in salads, and the seeds can be pickled like capers.

— **Japanese toad lily** (*Tricyrtis hirta*) is easy to grow in ordinary well-drained soil and forms great clumps. It is not fussy about light conditions, and is tolerant of a harsh winter. The flowers are star-shaped, speckled white and purple.

— **Yarrow** (*Achillea millefolium* 'Cerise Queen') is a vigorous perennial with a mass of pink flowers and a mat of dark green leaves. Yarrow also comes in reds and yellows, and tolerates alkaline soil.

Tropaeolum majus flourish in poor soil beneath hoardings on a roundabout in Elephant & Castle, London.

Alkaline-tolerant plants If you are gardening where a building once stood, or in a soil that resembles builder's rubble, the mortar will make it alkaline and therefore poisonous to some plants. The following plants are not troubled by the high pH:

— **English or pot marigolds** (*Calendula officinalis*) are remarkable. Bushy, fast-growing, and bearing orange and yellow daisy flowers for months, they can tolerate very acid and very alkaline soils and are some of the most versatile medicinal plants. They ease skin problems, treat fevers and bleach hair, and a tea brewed from the petals is thought by some to improve circulation.

— **Spindle trees** (*Euonymous fortunei*) are low-maintenance and versatile. Evergreen but multicoloured in yellows, whites, reds or greens, they work well as hedging or ground cover.

— **Lilacs** (*Syringa vulgaris*) are splendid deciduous shrubs that particularly like alkaline soil. Their huge tubular flowers in purple to pink and everything in between look like beehive haircuts. Since 1919 the lilac has been the state flower for New Hampshire, USA, because it is 'symbolic of that hardy character of the men and women of the Granite State'. A resident from there sent me money specifically to plant a lilac in London – a pink *Syringa vulgaris* 'Prince Wolkonsky' is now thriving in Elephant & Castle.

Wind-resistant plants Public space is often exposed to wind and the constant whoosh of traffic. This battering calls for plants with grassy and fine leaves, which can be used to shelter more tender plants behind them:

— **Juniper** (*Juniperus scopulorum* 'Rocky Mountain') is a tree with needle-like leaves that grow flat on the reddish-brown bark. It tolerates a wide variety of conditions, including hot sun.

— Forsythia (*Forsythia* 'Beatrix Farrand') is a vigorous deciduous shrub that blooms profusely with deep yellow flowers in early spring, and grows to a bushy 2m (7ft).
— Orchard grass (*Dactylis glomerata*) is a densely tufted, clump-forming grass with variegated leaves that runs rampant.

Salt-resistant plants In areas prone to snow and ice, roads are often gritted with salt. If your guerrilla garden is situated close to one of these poisonous highways, consider using plants suited to the unnatural environment.

— Kohuhu (*Pittosporum tenuifolium*) are evergreen shrubs with attractive glossy leaves of all colours ('Abbotsbury Gold' is yellow, 'Tom Thumb' is purple, 'Margaret Turnball' is dark green) and honey-scented flowers. They are frost-hardy and tolerate full sun or partial shade.
— Osteospermum (*Osteospermum jucundum*) forms neat, long-lasting evergreen spreading clumps with big daisy-like flowers in all sorts of colours from late spring to autumn.
— Beard tongue (*Penstemon digitalis*) has trumpet-shaped flowers in early summer, on stems 1.5m (5ft) high. It comes in many colours, and is a vigorous herbaceous perennial that tolerates salty conditions and survives with very little water.

INVASIVE PLANTING

To succeed in combat with minimum effort, choose weapons that continue to strike long after they are first deployed, spreading themselves far and wide without further intervention. The convenience of such plants comes with risks, however. Their invasiveness can overwhelm the environment in which you planted them, out-competing everything else, and you may end up fighting against them to protect other plants.

If using an invasive plant be particularly careful to choose one that is native to your environment. If it is not, there is a risk that it will unbalance the area's ecology and damage existing species. Consider the rampant azaleas (*Rhododendron ponticum*) of Wales. Shipped from their native regions in Asia to Britain in the nineteenth century, they loved their new home so much that they slipped over the garden wall, advancing in dense towering swathes across the hills of north Wales and beyond, killing off native species as they spread. Deploy invasive guerrilla plants only when you are confident you can contain them.

Underground plants Roots and rhizomes advance a plant in block formation, creating a front line as long as there is space:

— **Spearmint** (*Mentha spicata*), available in a variety of different minty flavours and shades of green, is so rampant that many people restrict it to a tub, either freestanding or buried in the ground. Plant it in open soil and its roots will spread far and wide, sprouting a dense sea of lance-shaped leaves. It is fully hardy and tolerant of poor soil.

— **Montbretia** (*Crocosmia* x *crocosmiiflora*) is a hardy plant that year after year shoots up spiky green leaves in springtime and in late summer produces spikes dotted with tiny, funnel-shaped orange flowers. It spreads rampantly in clumps.

— **Mallow bindweed** (*Convolvulus althaeoides*) is a perennial that clambers across the ground, over other shrubs, up fences and in poor soils to the point of being painfully invasive (hence the name bindweed). But the wide, funnel-shaped pink flowers in mid- to late summer provide a splendid display.

Aerial plants Seeds blown by the wind or dropped by animals will travel further and flourish whenever they land in an amenable setting:

— **Californian poppy** (*Eschscholzia californica*) will grow in gravel and poor soils, bearing a bright orange shallow-cupped flower in the summer from a low mat of fine hairy leaves. This annual will seed itself easily and return year after year.

— **Cosmos** (*Cosmos bipinnatus* 'Sonata Series') is another self-seeding and therefore self-perpetuating annual with large, showy, bowl-shaped flowers in white and pink on 30cm (1ft) stems. It tolerates exposed situations, not a lot of water and alkaline soils. Larger varieties that grow to 1.5m (5ft) are available too.

— **Butterfly plants** (*Buddleia davidii*) grow in the most barren of conditions and so spring up almost anywhere, rooting in a mortar crack high in a wall or across an almost soil-less pile of rubble. The arching twiggy shoots sprout lance-shaped leaves and lilac-style flowers 30cm (1ft) long from summer to autumn. They are a pioneering plant, leading the march across abandoned land. While the common *B. davidii* is deciduous, consider growing an evergreen species such as *B. asiatica* or *B. auriculata*, which both have white flowers.

DEFENSIVE PLANTING

A guerrilla gardener will be fighting a battle on several fronts that need defending. While there is no plant that will prevent a bulldozer coming in and razing your patch, fortunately this threat to a guerrilla garden is rare, and plants can be used to guard against more common invaders. We share the threats of weeds and pests with regular gardeners, but in public space we must also confront the problem of stray pedestrians.

Plant walls Plants can be used as deterrents to those who would otherwise use neglected land as a short cut, urinal or rubbish dump. Guerrilla gardeners who have opted to sacrifice open public access for the sake of more organized and sustainable community enjoyment choose to build permanent barriers. For other guerrillas the green barrier is an appropriate and cheap alternative to metal and one that still admits access for the most determined wanderer or fellow guerrilla. These leafy walls are best grown from evergreen shrubs or trees with prickly leaves, and can be very decorative:

— **Barberry** (*Berberis* x *stenophylla*) has spiky leaves and spiky stems all year round and a bonus of yellow flowers and blue berries. It is hardy, tolerates almost any soil and will grow up to 3m (10ft) tall.
— **Firethorn** (*Pyracantha atalantioides*) bears bright orange-red berries at the end of the summer, while the toothed leaves on the bush and thick vigorous growth form a defensive barrier of up to 6m (20ft).
— **English holly** (*Ilex aquifolium*) is a traditional Christmas decoration but can be enjoyed all year round. This shrubby tree has spiny, dark green leaves and can grow up to 25m (82ft) tall.

Weed-suppressing plants If you do not have time to weed your patch regularly, use plants that will battle hard against invaders by forming a pretty mat of colour:

— **Cranesbill** (*Geranium* 'Johnson's Blue') grows in a dense spread of lobed leaves flowering with saucer-shaped lavender-blue flowers in spring and summer. It forms clumps up to 75cm (2½ft) wide and is tough for any weed to take root in.
— **Bugle** (*Ajuga reptans* 'Multicolour') creeps across the ground for up to 1m (3ft) with a mat of dark bronze-green leaves speckled with cream and pink. It prefers moist and semi-shady conditions to full sunshine.

— **English ivy** (*Hedera helix*) is better known as a rampant wall cover, but it can also be used as a thick horizontal mat, even in dry soils. The 'Glacier' variety has grey-green variegated leaves and spreads up to 2m (7ft).

Plants for fighting pests Avoid the need to chemically spray your plants by using species that attract natural predators such as hoverflies, lacewing and ladybirds, which will pounce on pesky aphids and mites:

— **Marigolds** (*Tagetes* 'Mischief', 'Hero', 'Safari', 'Voyager') are annuals with glorious yellow and burnt-orange pom-pom flower-heads that attract hoverflies, while their roots emit a substance that repels the potato root eelworm. Big varieties are commonly called African marigolds and small ones French. Both germinate easily from large seeds scattered in late spring, and tolerate alkaline soils.
— **Scorpion weed** (*Phacelia tancetifolia*) is an annual that attracts hoverflies with its blue and lavender-coloured bell-shaped flowers. It is happy on stony, scrubby land in full sunshine.
— **Poached egg plant** (*Limnanthes douglasii*) is a brilliant annual that not only attracts bees and hoverflies but self-seeds freely and grows in scrappy places, producing in early summer a spillage of cupped flowers that look like miniature poached eggs.

PRODUCTIVE PLANTING

A fully productive vegetable guerrilla garden that will give a year-round crop requires environmental conditions similar to those of a private garden – which means a regular water supply, rich soil and protective devices to shelter plants from the weather, infestation and thieving. There are hundreds of guerrilla gardens like this, mostly those that have become official community gardens with good security and amenities to support the crops. Small-scale vegetable-growing is still perfectly possible in less hospitable places. Do be mindful, though, of potentially poisonous environments.

Tolerant plants Some vegetables do perfectly well in ground that still bears the scars of neglect, such as compacted sub-soil, nutrient deficiency and irregular watering.

— **Potatoes** (*Solanum tuberosum*) are the perfect crop for a vegetable patch on waste ground. Not only do they grow happily in previously uncultivated soil but they also improve the land as they do so by breaking up compacted earth. They are a good first crop for any guerrilla gardener to grow. If you have limited space go for a variety that is dug up early in the season, such as 'Pentland Javelin' or 'Epicure'.

— **Swiss chard** (*Beta vulgaris* var. *cicla*) is very easy to grow from seed in poor soil, and needs little attention; it even withstands light frosts. The leaves are rich in vitamins and nutrients and are best enjoyed young in salads.

— **Onions** (*Allium cepa*) are relatively easy to grow in any well-draining soil, and benefit from being planted in soil that has not been dug over for a while as it reduces their vulnerability to onion fly. A rich, regularly watered soil means a bigger, juicier onion, but if you can tolerate less impressive specimens on your plate the onion will accommodate less-than-ideal growing conditions.

Defensive plants Some edible plants succeed in deterring destruction and opportunistic thieving better than others by employing a variety of defensive techniques.

— **Salad radishes** (*Raphanus sativus* 'Cherry Belle', 'Scarlet Globe') are buried underground and grow very rapidly. They are ready

to harvest just four weeks after sowing. Although they prefer a reasonably fertile, well-drained soil, they are fairly tolerant of less favourable environments.

— **Blackberries** (*Rubus fruticosus*) bear delicious fruits to reward only those who have time to weave their hands carefully through the plant's thorny brambles. They are also thoroughly self-sufficient and can be found growing wild throughout Britain. Full sun and well-drained but moist soil at the base of a sheltered wall are optimum conditions, but not essential.

— **Broad beans** (*Vica faba*) can be trained to grow high up fences out of the reach of passing trouble. They appreciate a sunny location but are fairly drought-resistant and tolerant of most soils. Not only are they a productive vegetable, but they also enrich the soil by fixing nitrogen in it with bacteria in their root nodules.

SOURCING PLANTS

Planting in public requires generosity or frugality. Your floral bullets are left for all to enjoy but also for all to destroy. A new guerrilla gardener is likely to feel nervous about this and reluctant to invest much in plants that are going to be vulnerable to all kinds of enemies. As it is probable that you will have casualties, do not put your most precious troops in the front line until you are fairly sure of success.

Unless you are happy to throw money away I encourage the guerrilla gardener to find a good supply of cheap plants. Any fighter needs ready access to armaments, and you are no different. You may be fortunate to have your own garden as a munitions factory spewing forth seedlings and cuttings. If not, look further afield for an ally – a generous neighbour, a garden centre with spare plants or strangers who visit your website. Lora 3082 in Lethbridge, Alberta, even had bags of compost dumped by strangers on her guerrilla garden once word got around. As your confidence in your ability to hold a territory grows, you can upgrade to more sophisticated, expensive plants. Take anything offered to you for free, particularly in the early days of a dig, rather than dismissing it because it does not fit your planting scheme. Be resourceful and open-minded. As your supply of plants becomes more secure, you can always remove what you previously planted. Here are six good sources:

1. Your garden, if you have one, and those of allies are good bases in which to nurture delicate plants to maturity and from which to transplant unwanted self-sown seedlings and overgrown or tired plants to new guerrilla locations. Self-sown plants (which can be almost weed-like) are great because they are likely to be suited to your guerrilla plot and are helpfully low-maintenance.

2. Garden centres may sometimes have tatty plants to get rid of. While the plants are no longer sufficiently showy to be saleable they will still have plenty of life left in them. Herbaceous plants at the end of the summer or deciduous shrubs losing their leaves are your best-value bets.

3. Professional gardeners (even municipal ones) often have spare plants, most likely dug up to make way for new planting schemes. They find it cheaper to replace them with new plants from a nursery than to nurture them back to health for a new season. Getting rid of these is a guilty burden, so you will be doing them a favour if you can put the plants to good use.

4. Save seeds from food. Tomatoes (*Solanum lycopersicum*), peppers (*Capsicum annum*) and apples (*Malus domestica*) are commonly available in this way. Plant the seeds in little pots of earth, water them and cover in clear plastic wrapping until they sprout, then plant them out once the danger of frosts has passed.

5. An easy option, but one for which you will have to pay, is to go shopping. Depending on your access and budget, consider trade wholesalers and local shops. Seeds, sacks of bulbs and young plants can be good value here, and this option is quicker than tracking down allies and taking delivery of their donations.

6. Of course, in time, the best source of plants is from the ones you have grown already. They are eager to advance too, so help them along by harvesting seeds, dividing clumps and taking cuttings. Remember: your arsenal is alive.

Some troops at the extremist wing of the movement have suggested a Robin Hood approach to sourcing plants – i.e. steal from the rich to beautify areas for the poor. This I do not recommend. Not only is it theft, but you also leave behind a trail of destruction – quite the opposite of what we fight for.

5.2 Seed Bombs

Scattering seeds is the easiest way to guerrilla-garden. It is gardening in an instant, free from tools. Some plants will perish, some will flourish. You do not even need to stop moving to do it – Tony 830 releases handfuls of Welsh poppy (*Meconopsis cambrica*) seeds while driving along the M60 motorway near Barton Bridge, Lancashire. These yellow poppies will grow in both damp and dry conditions and are virulent self-seeders, ideal for carpet-bombing in this way.

Seeds must have soil and water to germinate, so they need to land in favourable conditions. If you are trying to turn a mountain of rubble and litter into something a bit more beautiful, just throwing seeds is not enough. Not only is the ground lacking the nutrients they need to grow, but lying bare will also expose them to drying by the sun and being nibbled by mice and birds. Using seed bombs is the smart approach, and there are several ways to build them.* These home-made dirty bombs assist germination by containing the additional ingredients of soil and water to help the seed get off to a good start, and are packaged like grenades so that they can be more easily fired into otherwise inaccessible places – be they behind fences or on terrain that is too dangerous to spend time cultivating.

Kathryn 079, a professor of art in California, has been seed-bombing since 1991 with avocado-shaped projectiles made by mixing and pressing together compost, native plant seeds and dextrin (a corn-starch derivative used as a binder in candy bars and cattle feed). She has mass-produced these, exhibited them in galleries, given them away[†] and thrown them around California at the start of the rainy season. Her inspiration came during a drought in Santa Barbara, when she saw the once beautiful landscape looking dead. She wanted to use her art to restore and celebrate natural systems.

Ella 1305 and Aimee 1306 have constructed an elaborate biodegradable device – a kind of seed shell – by sucking out the contents of a chicken's egg, pouring in wildflower seeds and a little compost and writing a message of hope on the outside.

More powerful forms of seed-bombing have been developed. Christopher 1594 in Richmond, Virginia, has devised the seed gun, which is a seed bomb that looks like a gun. He moulds them from red clay, organic compost, water and an assortment of seeds into the

* In 1973 the Green Guerillas put together what appear to be the first instructions for these. Donald 277 still circulates them and I have recently seen them republished. They suggest you fill old plastic balloons or glass Christmas tree baubles with seeds, peat moss, chemical fertilizer and water. These days most guerrilla gardeners have developed more environmentally-friendly methods.

† One of Kathryn's seed bombs was carried on to Jay Leno's NBC TV chat show by the actress Rene Russo in 2002. Whether Jay subsequently lobbed it anywhere around his neighbourhood of Tower Road, Beverly Hills, is not known.

shape of 9mm pistols (the weapon of choice for cops and criminals). A Danish collective developed the N55 Rocket System – a large weapon fuelled by a mixture of polyethylene and laughing gas that can be towed on the back of a bicycle.

If you are seed-bombing areas you do not intend to cultivate further, be mindful about matching the seeds to the native plant ecology of the area where they will be used; otherwise you risk disrupting the natural environment with an invasive new species.

5.3 Tools

The basic guerrilla gardener uses no tools – no specialist equipment is required to scatter seeds. But to make them more likely to grow it is worth aggravating the soil a bit first, because the seeds will root more easily in loose earth than in hard bare ground. Saddiq 754 uses a plastic fork, Girasol 829 uses a screw driver, but if you have access to specialist equipment I would advise you to start with a small metal fork. At the very least, scratch the surface; better still, dig it over. The fork is the first tool for a guerrilla gardener. A step up is a trowel. Use this to dig generous holes for potted plants. These two tools are fine for small-scale attacks, planting small plants in good soil, burying bulbs and cultivating tree pits.

Guerrilla gardeners who want to make more of an impact and cultivate larger areas must add bigger tools to their arsenal. A very neglected patch may be strewn with rubble, covered in a thick tangle of weeds or compacted hard from years of baking sun, beating rain and stray pedestrians. To clear such a mess use a large border fork and spade. Start with the fork, loosening the soil, breaking up the hard clumps, and pulling out weeds, rocks and anything that isn't good soil with your hands. The spade is used to lift and turn the soil over, to aerate it and to stir in manure or compost.

Once you have dug the soil it is best to level it out, to prevent lakes forming after rain and to provide an even base for plants and seeds. A rake is simply dragged across the soil, though a fork is a reasonable substitute if you hold the prongs up so that they just skim the surface. For the finishing touch bring a stiff brush to sweep away the mud that will inevitably be flung by enthusiastic guerrillas.

If your gardening involves taming existing rampant growth, then you will need secateurs to slice through branches. The bigger the plant, the more serious the slicing equipment you will need – Sam 076 helped me make light work of an overgrown butterfly bush (*Buddleia davidii*) in Elephant & Castle with his chainsaw. (Powered equipment is not really necessary for most guerrilla gardeners, and it takes away the pleasure of doing battle with manual weaponry.)

Invest in good-quality tools. In a big hardware store you will see a range that varies hugely in price. The first time I needed tools I bought cheap ones, but they did not survive long battling against compacted soil, unexpected lumps of concrete and being lugged around London. My Mother 008 lent me a spade and fork that had once been my grandfather's but these 50-year-old implements lasted five minutes before snapping. Choose something heavy-duty and with comfortable handles; they might seem expensive but should last a lifetime. Shop second-hand if you can. It is easy to tell good quality from poor: good-quality tools should feel weighty and produce a resounding clonk when struck.* Carrying and storing these heavy tools can be inconvenient for some guerrillas, so try to find somewhere near by – Julia 013 persuaded a coffee shop to look after hers. This kind of favour is reasonable to ask and is a way of involving local people who are keen to help in other ways than gardening.

---

* There should be no need to use your tools for any activity other than gardening, but it cannot be denied that like any well-stocked arsenal they may act as a deterrent to an aggressor. This provides a little reassurance when gardening in an unnerving public location.

5.4 Chemicals

Many gardeners are experts in chemical warfare. They enjoy pumping plants with synthetically produced cocktails of NPK (nitrogen, phosphorus, potassium) to create mind-blowing displays of acid-bright flowers and bloated vegetables like muscle-men gorged on steroids. Katie 1111 boosts clumps of the civic displays around her village of Otterton in Devon with a potent tipple, but she mischievously treats only half the plants so that she can delight in the official gardener's confusion as to why some petunias (*Petunia x hybrida*) grow bigger than others. However, there are many natural alternatives that will give your plants the head rush they need to charge into battle and flourish.

COMPOST
If you have space in your garden, build a compost heap in a sunny corner and recycle your garden waste (all vegetation except weeds with ripe seeds and very woody stuff) into a sweet-smelling stoke pile. Ideally sit the heap in a lidded box. To deter rats from making it their home, do not compost cooked food and keep the container as impenetrable as possible. In time dig it into the soil, which will enrich it with nutrients and improve water retention.

VERMICULTURE
Build a wormery. There are designs for these small plastic boxes that can be kept indoors – under a sink for example – without producing odours. Vermicomposting is therefore ideal for the urbanite without access to even a small piece of land. The worms, called red wigglers (*Eisenia fetida*), break down food waste into a nutrient-rich 'worm juice' fertilizer, and convert food scraps into a compost that can be applied directly to soil. The digestion in a worm's gut is performed by bacteria, so what it excretes is rich in beneficial microbial life.

LIVESTOCK

Larger guerrilla gardens might provide a home to domesticated livestock. The guerrillas of the Kinderbauernhof Mauerplatz, an 8,000-square-metre space in East Berlin, brought goats and chickens across the border from West Germany in the 1980s. Not only do the animals produce milk and eggs, but the waste they eat from the garden is returned as juicy manure. The garden's menagerie now includes rabbits and a pony, whose rotted excrement all goes towards making a powerful cocktail of chemical weaponry.

If you do not have space for your own animal-powered manure factory, find a local ready-made supply. There are still places in cities that have more manure than they know what to do with and give it away. Peter 509 in New York has collected bagloads of horse manure from his local police department. (Manure should not be used fresh on plants, but left to rot for several months to avoid scorching the greenery.)

5.5 Clothes

For basic guerrilla gardening you need to give no consideration to your outfit at all, as all you really need are your hands. The bare-knuckled guerrilla can adequately scatter seeds and pick up litter – but do wear *something*. Jerry 2821 sent me photos of him and his two friends guerrilla gardening in Brisbane wearing no more than a sweatband and necklace, which seems to be asking for trouble. Topless gardening for both men and women is permitted in Ontario, but I do not know of any female guerrilla gardeners taking advantage of this freedom to cool off when digging. We are dressing up neighbourhoods, so we should dress up too.

You do not need to wear an outrageous costume. The Guerrilla Girls, who were not gardeners but activists who mounted attacks on the art world, always dressed in a uniform of gorilla facemasks to disguise their identity, but we do not need to do that. Fancy dress is fun but it is likely to hamper effective gardening. A gorilla suit (fools have suggested it to me numerous times) would be unbearably hot, and a latex superhero outfit (also suggested) would ladder on contact with shrubs.

Although we are guerrillas, there is no reason to wear army camouflage. Looking like a soldier is only a good disguise if you are trying to blend in with troops in a bullet-filled war zone. There is also no need to follow Mao's clothing recommendation (two summer weight uniforms, one suit of winter clothing, two hats, a pair of puttees, a blanket, and an overcoat if you live in the north).

Your choice of battledress as a guerrilla gardener should reflect one of two approaches: either you disguise yourself, adapting the wardrobe of someone people would expect to see cultivating public space (a workman, a municipal gardener, a farmer if it is a rural dig), or you dress as casually as other members of the public. The first approach will require a few props. Helmut 1831 in the Netherlands and Stephen 1337 in Hampshire both garden in Day-Glo plastic jackets, the kind worn by safety-conscious street workers. A high-visibility jacket enables you to get away with all sorts of stuff. However, a word of caution. I tried this approach once and borrowed a fluorescent jacket as added protection while out late at night cutting a new bed for nasturtiums (*Tropaeolum majus*) in the tatty turf that covers the north roundabout in London's Elephant & Castle. By coincidence many other men in fluorescent jackets were also in the area that evening, busy renovating the nearby underground station. In theory my jacket and I should have blended into the Day-Glo blur of this official maintenance force, but I could not have been more conspicuous. While they were all wearing orange jackets, mine was yellow, and I was the centre of attention. A gang of four soon came over, curious to see what I was up to. I explained I was just gardening but they observantly enquired, 'Why is there a bus company's name across the back of your jacket?' Do not make my mistake – if you are going to assume a disguise do your research.

Personally, for most guerrilla gardening I favour the casual approach. When I am on regular maintenance missions to weed, collect litter and do a little planting I do not dress very differently from how I would normally. This means I can fit it in on my way to and from doing something else. If you are likely to be gardening, assemble your outfit with the practical common sense of a regular domestic gardener: wear something warm, breathable and comfortable. A hooded top would be eminently practical, except that in Britain, as the uniform of delinquent youths known as 'hoodies', it may provoke fear and aggression. You will want to stretch with your tools and kneel down in the dirt, so go for baggy and washable. Loose combat trousers (though please note my earlier comment about camouflage patterns) are well suited. Deep pockets are useful for shoving in a spare trowel, gloves, and other gardening odds and ends. Layers that can be removed and rolled into a bag are handy for when you get hot.

Consider what you look like when bending down. Adam 276 admits that he was first attracted to guerrilla gardening by the vision of Liz Christy's beautiful backside as she dug. Jim 006 came out gardening with baggy jeans and no belt and was frowned at for exposing his builder's bum. It would not matter in your back garden, but in public you must consider the effect of pulling revealing moves – it can distract passers-by and other gardeners.

Footwear requires the most thought if there is any chance you are going to be getting muddy. The most iconic of all gardening accessories, the Wellington boot, is technically best for the job. These calf-high rubber boots provide wading capacity in the muddiest of patches and a wonderful sense of being prepared for any terrain; they are the 4x4 for feet. But for the guerrilla gardener Wellingtons are only appropriate if you are dressing up as an official

or if you live in a rural market town where everyone wanders around in them. A practical and discreet alternative is the 'Wellington shoe'. Made from the same hard-wearing washable rubber, they are cut short at the ankle. I have a pair in sporty dark grey, which are equally at home masquerading as minimalist trainers in a nightclub as stomping on the flowerbed.

Old trainers are also fine. Obviously, avoid delicate shoes unless you can improvise additional protection for them. Andy 233 came to his first dig wearing an immaculate new pair of white trainers, but shielded them by wrapping his feet in two stray plastic carrier bags. He knew the bags could be whipped off in a moment and there would be no incriminating dirt on his shoes – and not even a footprint matching his tread.

Whether you are dressing as an official or going casual, there is one item you should always carry. It will mark you out in the street as a little different from passers-by but can be quickly removed and shoved in a pocket if you need to blend in. It is the essential pair of gloves – not any old pair but gloves designed specifically for gardening. I have seen guerrilla gardeners wear gloves designed for other purposes and fail. You will fumble sporting a thick pair of ski gloves and clog up woollen mittens with mud. Most hardware stores sell gloves for gardeners of all sensibilities, shapes and sizes, from slim-fitting cotton to chunky and rubberized. Take your pick.

Some guerrilla gardeners have designed a uniform for their troops. Stephanie 2487, a designer of recycled clothing, has made branded shirts for her Tree-0-5 group in Miami. Ben 2676 has printed T-shirts emblazoned with 'Guerrilla Gardener' for his family force of eight-year-old Lily 2677 and five-year-old Noor 2678. They provoked no curiosity when cultivating a neglected flowerbed in Crewkerne in Somerset, even though they were clearly labelled as guerrilla gardeners. (I expect the sight of two little children gardening had a disarming effect.)

Occasionally you may need to wear specialist clothing that will unavoidably make you stand out. Bee-keeping is popular on some large guerrilla gardens, but collecting the honey requires a big white body suit of protective clothing, including a facemask. Donald 277 was dressed up in one of these when two policemen passed by. Perhaps suspicious that he was handling dangerous chemicals, they needed some reassurance that his activity was peaceful; they left sharply when they realized that hanging around would get them stung.

5.6 Lights

If you guerrilla-garden at night you will need to think about light. Public space is often well illuminated and you may not need to supplement it. But if you do, wear a head torch as Sam 2798 and his Chicago troops do, as this will leave your hands free to garden. Lizzie 002 and Vicky 619 parked their car on the roadside so that it was facing the verge, and used the headlamps' blaze to light their tulip planting. (Make sure that the battery is well charged if you want to get home afterwards.) I know of one guerrilla in New York who toyed with the idea of tapping into a nearby lamp-post to power an extra light for his dark patch in the East Village. In the end he decided the risk of gardening in daylight was preferable to that of electrocution.

5.7 Communication

Carry a mobile phone. It is your link to back-up troops. Even in 1937 Mao saw this as vitally important: 'Guerrilla units must be equipped with some means of rapid communication.' His choice at the time was two-way radio, and by all means use this if you prefer.

5.8 Water

An old office water dispenser bottle is also a very capacious, robust and portable watering can.

You will need to consider the role of this precious resource in your guerrilla garden at an early stage. You may have decided to rely entirely on rainfall and planted accordingly. However, most gardens will need additional water at some point. Watering after planting also gives new plants a better chance of surviving. If you are fortunate enough to be within walking distance of a tap, then a standard watering can is fine and the issue is uncomplicated. In the United States, mains water can be legally intercepted from hydrants that stand on the sidewalk. Keys to them are readily available from hardware stores and permission can be obtained, if this is even necessary, to tap into the supply (Peter 509 gets an annual permit to water the Le Petit Versailles garden in New York). Many of us, however, do not have these luxuries. Roadside verges and abandoned lots tend to come without basic utilities.

Justin 1310 in Vancouver stretches a hose from his house on to his guerrilla garden in a derelict railway siding near Granville Island, despite being paralysed from the waist down. Margareeta 898 in Amsterdam has solved her water access problem by learning to pour a direct jet from her third-floor window on to her guerrilla tubs below. You may need to carry water over longer distances, but it is a heavy and potentially messy substance to transport. Les 847 in Vancouver has a pick-up truck with a 45-gallon drum on the back which he fills with water for spraying on to his guerrilla rose garden on drive-by missions, but, unlike him, most of us do not own a car-repair business with a fleet of specialist vehicles.

I began by carrying old petrol canisters – they hold five litres, are easily carried and keep their contents secure, but they alarm passers-by. One person saw me dousing my bed at St George's Circus in London with a cascade of clear liquid and shrieked at me, fearing I was about to set the garden on fire. Brigadier Peter 1532 in

Plymouth somehow manages to use a huge old military jerry-can without such trouble (perhaps because of his experience as a logistics expert, masterminding the supplies for the British Army's campaign in the Falkland Islands). Julie 159 offered me old plastic water bottles of the kind used in her office's drinks dispensers. I have seen these used by Stephanie 2487 in Miami with great success. They hold five gallons and are specifically designed to be lugged around by those unused to physical labour. If your patch is tiny, do as Lyla 1046 does and use an ordinary water bottle to pour water on to your bed as you pass by.

If your garden is big and secure enough, consider building a rainwater harvester. Try to intercept guttering off nearby roofs and collect the water in a butt. I helped Andy 343 and Bruce 2729 build a harvester in their Whitechapel guerrilla garden by tying a large plastic sheet along the top of a wall and below, so that it became a sloping plane which channelled rain into an old bath that had been conveniently dumped near by.

5.9 Transport

Mao writes that the guerrilla 'must move with the fluidity of water and the ease of the blowing wind'. Ideally, to flow with this grace the guerrilla gardener would use nothing more than their two legs. This way you remain footloose and free from the responsibilities of a vehicle – you are an infantryman rather than a cumbersome mounted cavalryman. As all fighters know, you do not want to be drawn too far from your home base or put the security of your supply route at risk. When your garden is a small plot of public space next to your home, getting there with your tools and materials is no trouble. Plants and equipment can be carried home from the shops or dropped round by friends; Naomi 272 has plants posted to her by mail order. But for anything more ambitious some form of transport is essential.

You will need transport to get to digs beyond your immediate environment and to carry more materials than you can manage by hand. A bicycle works well, making you almost as nimble as a pedestrian and offering the added advantage of a quick getaway. You can go anywhere, park anywhere and with a little ingenuity carry almost anything. Panniers and baskets are good for small tools and little plants; line them with old plastic bags to hold in the drips and dirt. Larger implements can be tied on to the frame of the simple pushbike. Andrew 1679 carries a spade around London in this way, and I have seen a film of guerrilla gardeners towing huge hornbeams (*Carpinus caroliniana*) in carts on the back of bicycles around San Francisco. Motorized two-wheeled transport offers the advantage of speed – Camilla 052 follows in the guerrilla motorcycle tradition of Che and comes gardening on her Suzuki SV650s super-bike.

Four wheels are better than two if you want to do really big stuff quickly. In the 1970s Liz Christy drove around New York in an old blue Datsun full of tools and materials to help other new guerrillas. I also use petrol-powered transport to get to bigger digs away from home and for collecting materials; hopefully the gardening activity facilitated by these carbon-emitting vehicles offsets their contribution to global warming.

Choice of vehicle is critical. You might expect a capacious estate car or truck to be most practical, but both have their drawbacks. When driving a rusty old green Volkswagen Golf I was pulled over by London's Metropolitan Police as a suspected terrorist and searched under the provisions of the Prevention of Terrorism Act 2005. My sacks of wood chippings piled up on the back seat were assumed by the twitchy officers to be a giant fertilizer bomb. The car was screaming out 'terrorist cliché'. A van, while disguising the innocuous contents from police view, has also been trouble for

me. I hired a large white Ford Transit to carry waste to a municipal dump, but the beefy staff (who had been friendly when I had gone there by car) turned mercenary and demanded a fee for what they now considered 'commercial' dumping – all because my vehicle had no side windows.

My most successful four-wheeled modes of transport have been old sports cars. Their leisurely image is an effective disguise for industrious activity and they usually have wide flat boots that are perfect for carrying trays of plants. I have found that a 1973 Volkswagen-Porsche 914 is particularly practical. Its mid-engine configuration gives it a boot at the front and the back, and there is space for a passenger or more equipment in the second seat. If you need to carry a high load the roof can be removed, making it perfect for transporting mature Christmas trees (*Picea abies*) and towering yuccas (*Yucca filamentosa*).

Public transport can be problematic for the armed guerrilla gardener. Gabriella 156 tried to travel from Slough to central London by train but had to abandon her spade because the guards considered it a dangerous implement. Go for more discreet hand tools. You can carry seeds on most forms of public transport (though leave them out of hand luggage on a plane), but large shrubs or dripping trays of seedlings will aggravate fellow passengers.

There are guerrilla gardeners who are not land-bound but have taken to the water, so forming our exclusive naval division. John Chapman, as a pioneering guerrilla gardener in the wilds of early nineteenth-century America, tied two dug-out canoes together to carry himself and his load of apple seeds along the Ohio River. More recently Al 466 has been using a seventeen-foot canoe. He paddles around the rivers near his home in Malton, North Yorkshire, collecting wood from the riverbanks. In return for this resource he plants young native trees there and in the surrounding countryside.

6. IN THE FIELD

You are now very nearly ready for action. It is time to get out there, scout for locations, gather your arsenal and get digging. The instructions in this chapter are compiled from field notes of guerrillas around the world, often in areas of urban neglect and public space, but are relevant to more rural locations and private space too.

In his guerrilla warfare manual Mao states, 'We must not attack an objective we are not certain of winning. We must confine our operations to relatively small areas and destroy the enemy and traitors in those places.' I totally agree (except for the bit about traitors, which I do not think is a problem for us). Simply avoid biting off more than you can chew. You can dream of a grand transformation but do not be in a rush to create it. It is basic military logic: do not advance into

Donald 2474 scattering *Digitalis purpurea* in Barons Court, London.

new territory until you have secured the ground you already hold. A guerrilla garden can very easily slip back into neglect if you take on something that is too difficult to maintain – whether because of the garden's scale, inhospitable terrain, lack of water or vulnerability to vandalism. In their hearts most guerrilla gardeners are idealists, but we need the measured pulse of a pragmatist too if our gardens are to flourish. This chapter is all about steadying that beat, and becoming a steely, successful guerrilla gardener in the field.

6.1 Choosing a Location

To a guerrilla gardener, nowhere is out of bounds – almost any landscape can offer potential in some way. But, strictly speaking, land you own or have permission to garden on is off limits – because here of course you are not a guerrilla gardener.

If your ambitions are modest the choice of location is fairly flexible. Scatter seeds more or less anywhere. Weeding and watering will greatly increase the chances that the seeds will bloom, but are not essential. Mining land with bulbs in autumn is even easier, because they grow when most weeds are dormant and the weather is naturally wetter. You usually need about five inches of soil to plant bulbs in. A deep hole and space to grow is fine for any native tree planted in spring or autumn; it will need little help after that if you stake it well – just water it generously if you have a prolonged dry spell in the first year. Another simple method is what Andy 287 calls the 'plant and plonk' strategy. He has brightened up his south London cul-de-sac by placing ready-planted flower boxes on the pavement outside his neighbours' homes.

But for a more ambitious garden the location becomes crucial. You can alter the land, but its context and intrinsic features will determine what grows, how the garden is used and how successful it is. Choose a location that you can easily get to. Somewhere near where you live or work is obviously helpful, for this and many other reasons. Regular maintenance (watering, litter collection, weeding) is much easier if you do not have to go out of your way and can spot in the course of your day-to-day life the tasks that need doing. Your arsenal will be close to hand. Gardening in your own community also strengthens your role in the area, your friendships with people and the likely support for the garden.

Choosing land that is publicly owned and publicly accessible is much more likely to lead to success, because you will not be trespassing and will perhaps be mistaken for a well-meaning public servant (which in a sense is what you are). Local authorities have many competing demands on their resources and may not mind you relieving them of some of the burden. Public organizations also have their reputations to worry about, and crushing a team of gardeners who are tidying up their local area has the potential to be very embarrassing.* By the time the owner of a piece of public land gets round to wondering whether your garden should be permitted or not it should be mature, blooming and politically a more difficult target to oppose than it would have been had you asked for permission when it was wasteland. The chances are they will never wonder at all. This kind of location comes in five key forms:

Verges, roundabouts and medians These are a strategic priority. They are likely to be neglected, lost between boundaries of responsibility and not good for much else. Planting here makes an

* The same is true of land occupations and guerrilla gardening in less developed countries. Anders 860 describes in his book *No Trespassing* (South End Press, 2000) how squatters in Peru and Brazil are more successful when they target public land, because public landowners are slower to gain eviction orders, by which time the occupiers are able to build a fully functioning neighbourhood. When squatters invaded the empty wasteland of Jardim São Carlos in Brazil, it was so successful that after a year the government supported them by building permanent homes and even a broom factory.

impact that can be appreciated by thousands every day. Add to or tidy up what is there, or else clear away the mess and build brand new beds, ensuring they are sufficiently obvious and edged to have a reasonable chance of avoiding the occasional mowing.

Tree pits Planting here complements the tree. Make space in the soil around the base of the trunk or, if the tree is tightly packed in with hard surfaces, build a raised bed around the tree. The tree will also benefit from you watering your plants.

Empty flowerbeds, planters and tubs These are yours to restore. You will probably find that beneath the surface of filth there is good soil, so less work is required to get the ground ready for planting. They are also usually positioned in impactful locations.

Beneath walls and fences These are a backdrop for climbing plants and also provide shelter. Because plants in these locations are more sheltered, they are more likely to survive the occasional strimming by municipal gardeners and trampling by pedestrians.

Derelict lots, railway sidings, demolished buildings Big sites like these provide the starting-point for community gardens that can be enjoyed as destinations in their own right, rather than just in passing. Start gardening within these intimidatingly large locations by making pockets of improvement, either around the fringes or as colourful, crater-like blasts across them.

It is possible to garden virtually anywhere – it is just a matter of how much effort you are prepared to invest in the transformation. Christian 3128 even led a troop of guerrilla gardeners on a mission to plant obsolete ash trays on Viennese U-Bahn platforms. Despite his signs encouraging people to water their 'Phoenix gardens',

Christian told me the plants did not last long – not because of the absence of natural light or the attentive Austrian police, but because they were pinched by elderly women.

6.2 Troops

Anyone can be a guerrilla gardener – you certainly do not need a military background.* It is the same for conventional guerrillas. Mao writes, 'As long as a person is willing to fight, his social condition or position are no consideration.' In Russia in the early 1920s, Soviet guerrillas included both 'silver-haired units' of old men as well as children in their ranks, and arming children as guerrilla fighters continues to this day. While it is uncomfortable to be reminded of this despicable exploitation of youngsters, we can once again learn from guerrillas. Unlike killing people, gardening really can and should be for anyone, and getting the young and old to participate in our battle is to be commended.

The youngest I have fought alongside was four-year-old Beatrice 2930 of Plymouth, and the oldest so far has been my 91-year-old grandmother Margot 623. Disabilities need not get in the way. Raised planters are wheelchair-accessible – Adam 276 has been building these in the Clinton Community Garden for injured US veterans. Sean 2350 is blind but he still manages to guerrilla-garden tree pits in his London street, using brightly coloured plants such as African daisies (*Osteospermum ecklonis*) and by feeling the leaves for turgidity to see when they need watering. You will find troops among friends and family, neighbours, local businesses,

---

* One of the first Lower East Side guerrilla gardeners was in the French Resistance, and she had a few assassinations under her belt, but such a lethal record is quite unnecessary. Nevertheless I was told she fought ferociously well into her eighties, determined to rid the world of modern-day Nazis and make New York more beautiful.

students, passers-by (including drunks), the media and, if you are really organized, those doing community service – Margaret 2878 used young offenders in Devon to repaint the wall of her churchyard garden.

If someone comes along showing willingness, make sure you channel this into competence. Direct a new and inexperienced volunteer towards less challenging tasks like turning over the soil and removing pebbles, and do not be shy about telling them what to do – they will be keen for instruction. Some people come guerrilla gardening because they want to learn how to grow something without the risk and embarrassment of killing plants of their own.

If you have initiated a dig, provide some leadership. On this subject Mao's observations on guerrilla warfare are once again directly relevant for guerrilla gardeners:

> *All guerrilla units must have political and military leadership . . . leaders who are unyielding in their policies – resolute, loyal, sincere and robust . . . unorganized guerrilla warfare cannot contribute to victory, and those who attack the movement as a combination of banditry and anarchism do not understand the nature of guerrilla action.*

A leader does not need to be a boss, and a guerrilla gardening group will flourish when the troops feel emancipated. The leader should help facilitate the group to develop their own ideas, discuss them and find common ground. Steve Frillmann, the current executive director of the Green Guerillas in New York (the incorporated not-for-profit organization that has evolved from the original group of activists) says that the most successful community gardens are those where a few basic principles are agreed in the early days, about why they are creating a garden and how they want to go about building it.

Some guerrilla gardeners can reach these conclusions without leadership. Julia 013 in Berlin says adamantly, 'We want the process of decision-making to stay in the group, we don't want leadership or anyone to make decisions for all.' In Buenos Aires Daniel 1224 reiterates this point and enjoys the flat structure of his community garden. Yet both Julia and Daniel have natural leadership qualities; I think they are perhaps just uncomfortable with the associations of carrying the badge. Do, of course, beware of becoming a dominant figure on whom troops rely too much, and avoid crudely imposing on a new territory a method that you have successfully implemented somewhere before. You need to be a pragmatic, enabling guide, not a dogmatic hound.

Troops are not even essential for the guerrilla gardener. Many guerrillas fight alone as free agents. These nimble independents lack the capacity for rapid, large-scale change and lose out on camaraderie, but they gain total control, discretion and spontaneity. Guerrilla gardening is perfectly practical as a solo effort. Just get out there and do it – too many potential guerrilla gardeners sit around discussing ideas or waiting for potential troops to find a convenient date. If you find people dawdling about participating, stop the talk and replace it with action. Later you can use your solo experience and success to win support for taking on larger territory and creating more spectacular gardens together.

6.3 Timing

The timing of your dig is crucial if you are to keep interruptions to a minimum while remaining visible to potential supporters. This is a fine balance to strike, and only good knowledge of your community's social terrain will enable you to judge when is best – if in doubt veer towards invisibility. The bigger the dig and the more of a spectacle you are, the more important timing becomes. Use out-of-hours periods to avoid confrontation with the worst of what I call 'pests' (more on these later). Angela 2585 in Milan first struck a roundabout at around 11pm, and Esther 418 in north London began her guerrilla gardening with the dawn chorus. In central London we have learnt that gardening between about 7.30pm and 10.30pm is most effective for avoiding trouble and meeting supporters. Weekends are preferable to weekdays. These times are also often the most convenient to guerrilla gardeners if they work regular hours.* As your confidence grows, and the positive impact of your activity becomes more visible, you can garden with less secrecy and dispense with the cloak of darkness.

If you are recruiting people you do not know, perhaps through a website or notices, you may feel that the event is a bit like a 'flash mob', as when complete strangers stage (for example) pillow fights in public at a precise, predetermined moment. Guerrilla gardening is not like this at all. We are not so disciplined or choreographed. Think of the evening as a party to which people bring their own potted plant rather than a bottle of wine, and come and go casually. You will have some anxious minutes at the start, worrying that no one else is going to come, but soon the dig will be in full swing. If it is a good evening, troops will stay late and come again.

The timing of a dig is much less important if it is a very small or solo mission. You can be spontaneous if you have a pocket full of

---

* Holidays are also worth considering, not just in your local area but when you are travelling too. I packed a trowel and went gardening in the streets of Tripoli, Libya, intent on meeting a few locals and encouraging them to get involved. While I dug an anonymous succulent into a neglected pavement planter, my travelling companions Mike 054 and Steve 007 stood by ready to intercept passers-by and reassure them of our peaceful motives. It turned out our dig was immediately outside the local Revolutionary Youth Council social club, and their leader Qaies 2408 took an enthusiastic interest in our activity. He invited us into the club, and with Colonel Gaddafi looking down from an imposing official portrait he enlisted at GuerrillaGardening.org, reassuring us he would take care of the plant.

seeds, or are passing a patch in need of a little litter clearance. Small numbers are less visible and more rapidly responsive to a surprise. Because the work is slower, this approach is best suited to small-scale digs or casual maintenance missions. These digs can be slotted into your day-to-day life with little trouble. Tom 2221, a postman in Amsterdam, showed me where he had planted sunflowers (*Helianthus annuus*) while doing his deliveries, planting in both public and private spaces. I slipped in a spot of guerrilla gardening between courses while visiting a friend in Zurich for dinner. Alice 122 and I took glasses of wine outside together with a bag of yellow tulips (*Tulipa* 'Golden Melody') and planted them next to a bus stop in Kornhausstrasse before returning indoors for pudding.

6.4 Soil

If you are growing a garden on soil that is already *in situ*, it is still worth considering adding ingredients to make it more fertile and better at retaining the right amount of water. Effort put in at the outset will pay off for a long time.

There are six basic soil types – clay, sandy, silty, peaty, chalky and loamy – which, unless your location is entirely dislocated from its environment, will correlate with the natural geology of the area. Other gardening books will give you more precise detail, but in principle add lots of well-rotted manure and organic matter, particularly if the soil is very sandy or very heavy and clay-like. To the latter you may also want to add sand.

A slightly acidic soil with average fertility and a high content of organic matter will satisfy the widest choice of flowers and vegetables. But if you are gardening where a building once stood, the chances are that it is quite alkaline because of limestone in the cement and mortar. This ground will benefit from the addition of lots of acidic

Purple 321 scrapes
horse manure from
the roadside in New
York's Central Park
in the early 1980s.

composting. Consider using plants tolerant of alkaline soils as well. You may need to import soil (Julia 013 carried in sacks from far outside Berlin, in a large trailer tied to the back of her bicycle). Although this is time-consuming, back-breaking work, it will provide you with a fertile, healthy base on which to build your garden.* Find out where construction work is happening, as you could be doing developers a favour by taking topsoil off their hands.

Some guerrilla gardeners go to extreme efforts to enrich the soil by making the most of waste. Between 1975 and 1980 at the impressive guerrilla Garden of Eden in New York, Purple 321 filled 15,000 square feet with manure made from horse droppings scraped from the trails of Central Park, and to enrich the soil further he reportedly recycled his own excrement.

Water retention and weed suppression can also be improved by covering the freshly turned earth with a layer of mulch. Wood chippings are ideal for this. Although sacks can be bought, it is more satisfying and ecologically responsible to reuse waste from garden pruning. In Dublin, Tampopo 2236 asked a local tree surgeon to give him shredded waste (which the surgeon would otherwise have had to pay to dispose of). Tampopo spread it around the tired old beds of Shirling Walk where he has been guerrilla gardening since 2005. It is not just good for the soil, he tells me, but the pine tree mulch smells good too.

Consider that in urban areas there may be high levels of toxins in the soil, ranging from heavy metals such as lead in old paint to pesticides and hydrocarbons. These contaminants can accumulate in plants, particularly root vegetables. If you are not intending to eat

---

* An alternative to digging the soil is to adopt the principles of permaculture. A full explanation of this approach is best sought elsewhere but I am aware that those who use permaculture methods believe soil is best enriched by adding layers of organic matter on top and letting natural processes do the mixing instead of you and a spade. Whether you are confident that plants benefit from this or not, a guerrilla gardener who wants maximum impact with minimum action should consider trying it. I, however, still enjoy slicing up the ground, turning the soil and getting a good look at what is lurking underneath.

the food, ignore it – there are bigger things to worry about; it is only a problem if nothing will grow at all. In New York, Zachary 922 tests soil to see if it is polluted, and if necessary uses ingenious bioremediation techniques to clean the land with living organisms; for example, oyster mushrooms (*Pleurotus ostreatus*) break down the toxins from oil.

6.5 Litter and Treasure

Litter collection is a big part of guerrilla gardening. You may need to remove a lot of this before you even cut the earth. Do not imagine that digging it in will make it go away; thorough decontamination is essential.

Wear thick gloves and make sure you can see clearly what you are doing. Collecting litter never ends. Litter is magnetic: the more there is, the more it attracts. Some people stupidly think they are keeping streets tidy by dumping rubbish on flowerbeds rather than on the pavement. Do not encourage this by allowing litter to gather on the beds. Keep on top of it by removing or reusing anything whenever you see it. Look out for a bag floating around and use it as a glove and receptacle in the same way that dog walkers hygienically remove their pets' poops. Picking up other people's litter is something to do as visibly as possible (particularly if they have just dropped it). Expect to provoke looks of astonishment and big smiles from passers-by – it can even encourage them to do the same.

As you collect litter you can become an archaeologist and forensics expert, piecing together evidence of the historic and secret usage of the neglected space. You sometimes find hopeful signs in relics of vanished gardens – old plastic plant labels and pockets of dark peat where a long-gone plant once grew show potential for your patch. I have developed an interest in noting the varying popularity of different snack foods by location and by time, an anthropological investigation that is easy because so much packaging is totally un-biodegradable. Knives and discarded hypodermic needles in flowerbeds are depressing discoveries indicating especially unhealthy habits in your area.

Litter can be disposed of where it should have been in the first place – in a bin. Look out for a handy nearby skip or a giant residential dustbin to use, or else just leave the junk in thick sacks by the roadside for the bin men to remove. If you have transport, load up the car and take your rubbish to a local dump. I have ended many an evening's gardening with a visit to the 24-hour tip at Cringle Dock in the shadow of London's spectacular derelict Battersea Power Station. The atmosphere there is still electrifying.

Not everything needs to be thrown away. One man's rubbish is another man's gold. There is always the possibility of unearthing hidden treasure. In the Creative Little Garden, on New York's Sixth Street, guerrilla gardeners reused old bricks and architectural bric-a-brac for paths and borders. Stones can be used for rockeries, upturned bottles for pathways and plastic bottles as tree-watering funnels, while discarded timber can be reused as fencing or for building a compost heap or a raised bed. Sometimes the treasures are to take away and enjoy. I discovered a disc jockey's mixing desk hidden in a shrubbery outside Perronet House, and Gary 728 dug out a small toy wizard that he auctioned off to fund more gardening. It is amazing what you can unearth.

Donald 277 records perhaps the most incredible discovery. He was working his shovel in a deep hole in the Liz Christy garden when suddenly his work was lit up by a shaft of light coming from the base of the pit. He had dislodged a brick in the ceiling on the subway that ran directly beneath the garden and could spy the Sixth Avenue line below. It turned out that in some places the garden sits on no more than a foot and a half of soil. Donald did

Welland
odge
en Centre
TRAFFIC
CONTROL
WELLAN
Bars & Re
BARRAT
NEW HOM
SHOW
vds
POLICE
POLICE
POLICE

not leave the hole as a handy waste disposal chute but plugged it with bricks.

For some people, litter collection is the sole focus of their guerrilla activity. Jonathan 2168 is a photographer living in the Leicestershire village of Lubenham. He regularly walks along the main A4304 road to the town of Market Harborough, and one day he was struck by the spontaneous beauty of a magazine littering the roadside. He photographed it, and this became the start of both an art project and a massive litter collection scheme. Three years on he has exhibited his photographs in galleries around the country and – to the horror of his neighbour – collected enormous piles of rubbish in his back yard. Jonathan even washed, counted and weighed it all to discover that PepsiCo manufactured the most items and that council roadside repairs were responsible for half the weight.

If the prospect of clearing a mountain of litter is putting you off getting started, then consider getting someone else to do it. Try even working with the council on this one. Tom 354 got his local authority, Hammersmith and Fulham council, to clear the mountain of mattresses from a square in Barons Court, making the guerrilla gardening attack that followed a lot easier. In Brooklyn's Quincy Street residents identified a corner patch they wanted for a community garden. It was the site of a demolished house that the owner, Reverend Reed, had allowed to become a dumping ground for old cars. Sometimes cleanliness is not next to godliness, and this preacher ignored complaints about the pollution. The residents' first big protest action was to lie on the sidewalk in a visible sign of solidarity about the mess. This led to the city taking up their cause and billing Reed for thousands of dollars' worth of cleaning. When he refused to pay this, the land became public, and shortly afterwards gardening began legitimately, without any need for further guerrilla action.

26,675 pieces of litter weighing 946kg collected from just half a mile of the A4304 in Leicestershire by Jonathan 2168.

6.6 Pests

Mao compared guerrilla units to 'innumerable gnats'. I disagree. Guerrilla gardeners are not gnats, and our attacks on the landscape are not pesky, irritating bite-marks. We have our own pests to deal with. First of course there are the usual four-or-more-legged irritants every gardener endures: bugs, flies, vermin and larger creatures. Other gardening books will give you more instruction on how best to deal with all of these – try ingenious tricks like a 'slug pub' (a submerged deep carton of beer for slugs to drown in) or a layer of sharp crushed eggshell to deter snails, and so on. However, the main pests a guerrilla gardener must deal with in the field are two-legged mammals (and I do not mean gorillas).

AUTHORITIES AND LANDOWNERS

Gardening on land that is not yours without permission puts you in direct conflict with the landowner and those who are employed to enforce rules. While trespassing is only an issue if the land is private, gardening on any land without permission is seen as vandalism – in the UK it is defined as 'criminal damage'. Potentially you are creating obstruction, defacement, pollution and disorder – which is not the intention of most guerrilla gardeners, but some less enlightened onlookers may not know that. Horticultural consultants, sanitation department employees and highway maintenance managers usually spell trouble because your work overlaps with their job and confuses them. The police may be trouble because they are there to uphold society's rules and you are breaking them. Landowners may of course object to you intervening in their space without permission.

Try to avoid confrontation, particularly in the early days when you have little to show for your efforts. Che learnt how going unwashed for days gave his troops an invisible shield: 'Our bodies gave off a peculiar and offensive odour that repelled anyone who came near.' I suggest other methods for keeping a low profile. Timing your attack out of hours helps. Avoid conversation with official-looking people, but if they initiate it be straightforward. Tell them you are gardening, because they may assume that you are doing anything but this – burying, hiding, stealing or mindlessly destroying. Say you want to make the area more attractive and that you are a volunteer. This is extremely difficult for anyone to take issue with (although if you are surrounded by piles of mud where there was once a superficially tidy area they may need more convincing).

Even if your motivations are more political – the area should be yours, you are angry it is a mess, you are starving and tired – do not aggravate the pest by telling them so. Like wasps they will sting. Tempting though it may be to give a smart response, I recommend avoiding doing so until you can see they are already your friends. (Gerrard Winstanley did not help his gardening cause in 1649 by being too casual with Sir Thomas Fairfax – Lord General of the Commonwealth no less – by refusing to take his hat off and addressing him as 'Tom'.) Bite your lip and be polite. Stay calm, do not do anything sudden, make them feel relaxed, and smile.

I have had several encounters with the authorities when caught red-handed – or should that be green-fingered? The most frustrating was with a street cleaner in Southwark while gardening one Saturday afternoon (foolishly visible). The confrontation was about 'my' use of 'his' rubbish bins. I regularly cleared litter from the neighbouring flowerbeds into these bins, as this was not part of his job remit. When he saw me putting litter in the bins (including some garden waste) he challenged me: 'You're filling them up too quickly.' I tried to reassure him that in our own way we were doing the same job and pointed out that I was not in control of how much litter needed clearing, but he seemed unsatisfied. The next morning I found the entire contents of one rubbish bin emptied over my freshly sown seedbed. The situation was resolved when the local newspaper picked up the story – 'Guerrilla Gardener Goes Ape,' screamed the headline – and since then Southwark council seem to have been shamed into accepting my free rubbish collection.

Unlike contractors, police and security guards are around in the evening, but trouble from them is rare. Even if it is not immediately apparent, remember again to tell them you are making the area cleaner and more attractive. A clear conversation will usually be sufficiently reassuring that your action is commendable or at worst barely significant. In London we have had police vans pull up and officers linger for a chat. One uniformed duo arrived with lights flashing and siren blaring – called out on suspicion that I was stealing plants – but I showed the officers that my tub was full of dandelions (*Taraxacum officinale*). Luckily for me they recognized weeds and, looking puzzled (I was gardening alone at 12.30am), let me continue.

My most serious problem with the police was while driving to a dig. They pulled me over under the 2005 Prevention of Terrorism Act, suspecting my car was laden with high-explosive fertilizer (it could have been, but that day it was wood chipping mulch). In Brussels, Girasol 829 and his troops were encircled by anxious guards after a tip-off from the American Embassy – someone had spotted them prodding the ground near by with screwdrivers. Neither Girasol nor I was interned. More recently, passing police have recognized us as guerrilla gardeners and quite happily shared a cup of tea and supported what we were doing (though they have not yet dug alongside us). Generally they have more serious disturbances to deal with.

There are some officials who are very serious trouble for guerrilla gardeners. Their sole responsibility is to undermine and obstruct common sense; they expect the worst from people and spend their time looking for opportunities to prove their point. They are the small-minded jobsworths whose roles in their organizations are so small and pointless that they have nothing better to do than get in our way. In the summer of 2005, 58-year-old Malcolm 332 had a serious confrontation with one such person. Malcolm lives in Bradlands, in Oxford, a suburban close of 1960s flats set around a communal lawn. He was already an award-winning gardener for his private patch but was disappointed that his high standards were not matched by the shared space. He set about removing litter and dog mess, mowing the lawn, clearing weeds, maintaining hanging baskets and painting bollards.

Unfortunately the local council's Crime and Nuisance Action Team (CANAcT) found out about this and, after what they described in the local press as 'a lengthy and costly investigation', issued him with a notice banning him from a long list of specific activities, including mowing the lawn, making compost, having bonfires and growing vegetables in communal areas. Should he want to help a neighbour he was instructed to lodge that person's written consent at the CANAcT offices. Apparently one neighbour had complained to the council, but this misguided grass was hugely outnumbered by the supportive locals who rushed to his side after CANAcT issued their notice.

Malcolm entered into a battle of foul play and spin. When the council found a dead rat in his compost heap, Malcolm (suspicious it was filthy sabotage) employed an expert from Oxford University to certify that his composting was not a health hazard. The battle spread into the local media, and Malcolm adeptly whipped up support for his cause – so much so that a mysterious benefactor in a white Rolls Royce glided into his estate and promised him a new lawn mower. The pesky council was eventually shamed into allowing Malcolm to continue.

The fight with authorities is never over, even when you think you have official permission. The guerrilla gardeners of New York thought their street-fighting days were well behind them by the mid-1990s. While a few gardens had been bulldozed over the years, most had become legitimized after the gardeners agreed to pay a nominal rent to the Department of Housing Preservation and Development. They were also supported by a publicly funded organization called Green Thumb. But the political landscape changed in 1997, when Mayor Giuliani set about auctioning off 300 of the gardens. What were once seemingly worthless patches of land had become ripe for development. Mass protests that extended far beyond the gardeners saved many old guerrilla gardens during this period, but the fight continues.

As I write, the fifteen-year-old Pueblo Unido garden in Harlem has been smashed up to make way for luxury apartments. On a notably unlucky Friday 13th in April 2007, local people spotted contractors hacking away at the shrubs in their garden, and when the latter were asked what they were up to they first lied, saying it was their garden, and then refused to say on whose behalf they were working. The gardeners called the police, but the contractors refused to explain what they had been doing and left silently in their trucks. Unfortunately the damage had been done. Aresh 1451, who fights to protect gardens across New York, tallied the destruction. All but one severely damaged peach tree (*Prunus persica*) had been flattened. Gone were four other mature trees, four rose bushes (*Rosa* spp.), a tool shed, garden furniture, a barbecue pit and the basketball hoop and stand. Such illegal pre-emptive strikes by contractors are designed to sap willpower. In the words of the local pastor Michael Vincent Crea, 'This was truly a terrorist act.' The gardeners have vowed to fight on and restore the garden.

Ideally, guerrillas should get to their garden before the contractors and their power tools rock up. You can even live there when times are desperate. Zachary 922 builds what he calls Garden Defence Mechanisms. One of these, in the More Senior Garden, New York, is a hammock-like nest 36 feet up a maidenhair tree (*Ginkgo biloba*), to which two people can climb up should the garden be threatened. Despite this infrastructure the garden was bulldozed in October 2003 – even its chicken coop was flattened. Zachary and the More Gardens Coalition decided to retake the garden. He invaded at night with home-made, pre-fabricated parts of a casita,* in which he and other defensive forces camped until the very end of December. When the police came, the gardeners put chains around their wrists and clipped themselves on to 'sleeping dragons'† deep in the ground. A sleeping dragon is very hard for anyone to extract you from, delaying eviction and giving time for the media to arrive and record the attack – which you hope will be reported in your favour.

Zachary is realistic about the tactics. 'In the end it may not save that garden, but it saves others earlier in the demolition process. It all kind of works synergistically, gets people interested, draws attention to community gardens.' He now responds to cries for help from other gardens under threat and helps gardeners unite and defend themselves with training and direct action.

THIEVES AND VANDALS

'What are you doing? Won't that all get pinched by the morning?' has been the reaction of miserable, sceptical passers-by when they see us installing showy new plants where before there existed nothing. In most cases their pessimism is unfounded, the plants becoming a visible sign that their community is not as bad as they thought it was. But I cannot deny that thieves and vandals are a problem when gardening in publicly accessible space. There is a direct correlation between plant loss and a poor weeding and litter clearing regime. If you fail to keep on top of these tasks and the

---

* A casita is a small shelter, typically built by guerrilla fighters when they want something more substantial than a basic tent or alfresco living.
† A sleeping dragon is a pipe cemented downwards into the ground with a strong crosspiece at the base. With a rope and carabiner around your wrist you clip yourself to the crosspiece and hold your ground. No one but you can release the contraption.

garden starts looking unloved, it is my occasional experience (and I think quite reasonable to expect) that the plants growing in this mess will be 'liberated' by eager gardeners.

Even with a good regime in place you are vulnerable to attack. Two years in a row now my great big red poppy (*Papaver orientale*) outside Perronet House has been torn from its stem almost as soon as it has bloomed. Luc 158 in Montreal, who plants a long, L-shaped bed at the foot of a pavement wall along Sherbrooke East, suffers an attack at the same time each year. Andrew 1679 had a Washington palm (*Washingtonia robusta*) and a Scots pine (*Pinus sylvestris*) stolen from a bed in Hackney. We take such thefts on the chin, as disappointing but acceptable losses in battle.

Matt 1764 and Jennifer 1765 in Fillmore Street, San Francisco, have learnt to find fun in the ups and downs of their street-side guerrilla gardening. A vandal rips up their wild flowers in the tree pits and destroys their fencing, but they call their creepy pest the Grumple. They say 'for every act of vandalism he does we are coming back with double the amount of love ... if you are going to do this you have to stay strong. The amount of good the flowers do far outweighs the pain caused by the Grumple.' They even turn their ripped and strewn wildflowers into bouquets to take home.

Adam 276 in New York does not take it on the chin; he fights back. When one vandal peed on his flowers, he retaliated by directing his own powerful mains-plumbed hosepipe directly into the offending man's open-top BMW. Now Adam has installed a defence against urination – a piece of clear plastic sheeting that he proudly calls the 'piss panel'.

If you cannot face the battle head on, what you can do is make your garden less obviously showy. Dramatic, exotic plants attract attention, so if you use them try to do so where pedestrians are less likely to linger or reach over. Or, plant them en masse, so that one does not stand out as a tempting beacon, and so that you can afford to lose some. To protect her plants Margaret 2878 hides them! In a crevice between a wall and gravestones in her churchyard garden she has planted a valuable hedge of hazelnuts (*Corylus avellana*) and blackberries (*Rubus fruticosus*) that will be a good, strong metre high before they are clearly visible. Mining an area by digging in bulbs is invisible and gives reasonable protection to the source of your improvement. Although their floral explosions may be picked, they will resolutely come back each year unless your pest is determined enough to dig them out. Be encouraged by the words of Chance the gardener from the Oscar-winning horticultural comedy *Being There*: 'As long as the roots are not severed all is well. And all will be well in the garden.'

DRUNKS

If you venture to areas of notorious urban neglect at night you will probably find some people loitering there in a state of personal neglect. A troop of guerrilla gardeners will not go unnoticed by them. If you are doing more than a quick seed bombing I recommend that at least one of you is familiar with the area – perhaps the patch is the rough corner at the end of your street, or you know the pub near by. I spoke to Hayley 2050, one of a well-meaning but naive nocturnal force of young female guerrillas in Bournemouth. She got chased away by local yobs when she was on a mission guerrilla gardening around a housing estate on the other side of town. One drunk at Manor House in north London insisted on demonstrating how our new bed of lavender (*Lavandula angustifolia*) would make a splendid scented mattress for him to take a nap on. Fortunately he eventually got bored – and lavender is very forgiving.

The most obstructive interference I have had was from a huge drunk delighted to find a troupe of twenty or so gardeners to entertain him on Westminster Bridge Road, particularly as some were buxom and sweaty. He sat down next to Sarah 288, an

Australian nanny, and told her she was 'the nicest princess I have ever seen'. She did not seem enthusiastic, so I stepped in. Occasions like this require choice phrases. A form of mild terror works best: 'I'm on community service, my parole officer will be here in a moment', or 'This area we're digging is heavily polluted with lead and asbestos.' I have noticed there is a strong correlation between a vagrant lifestyle and religious superstition, so I tend to use 'My dad's a vicar.' This line also works well with the police, and you are welcome to borrow it.

Alternatively, if you are calm and clear about what you are doing with them, there is a chance that drunks can be recruited to garden. Point them in the direction of a simple manual task, such as turning the soil over or filling bags with weeds, and keep an eye on them. While gardening in Hackney in London I met Alexander 2237. He was on his own that evening and seemed distracted by the vision of Naomi 272 and Lita 610 forking the ground. They were comfortable with him and it took little encouragement to get him to join us gardening. For an hour he turned over the soil like a demon, finding huge contentment in losing himself in a world of mud, and he handed back his spade a satisfied, exhausted man. We were only a little taken back when he asked for payment – 'Enough for a can of beer, please' – but this seemed like a fair trade for a mercenary. If a drunk feels that the garden is partly their achievement, there is a chance that they will not only look after it but also defend it from destructive friends.

DOG OWNERS

There is place for dogs within our ranks. On a dig in public space, a well-trained animal can provide comfort, defence and a conversation starter with passers-by. But while dogs may be man's best friend, their owners are pests. Think about where owners are most likely to allow their pooch's pungent payloads to be dropped. A guerrilla

gardener sees a tree pit as a potential flowerbed; a dog owner sees it as a pet urinal. Wear gloves in prime sites. Try putting up signs suggesting owners take their dogs elsewhere.

There is always a risk that the owners will fight back. One spring day, Torgut 1561 and his friends were tending his Jerusalem artichokes (*Helianthus tuberosus*) on the junction of Richard Sorge Strasse and Mühsam Strasse* in Berlin when the burly shaven-headed owner of two big dogs approached him aggressively. This man felt that the gardening was a protest against his dogs pooping in the street. He grabbed a shovel, pushed Torgut to the ground and threatened him with the tool. The police arrived but the thug had already left, shouting, 'I'll pull up your plants in the night.' Despairingly the gardeners erected a sign declaring their peaceful intentions, and to date they have escaped damage.

Because dog owners cannot be relied upon to ensure their pets are considerate, consider protecting your garden. Guerrilla gardeners in New York erected fences around their plots as soon as they could, to protect against theft as well as canines. Today, few guerrilla gardens in Manhattan admit dogs – fortunately, elsewhere in the city dogs are catered for with specific runs. In Berlin, Julia 013 has satisfied dog owners' demand for green space by partitioning the Rosa Rose Garden with a tall fence. The gardeners have one side, the dogs and their owners the other.

OTHER GUERRILLA GARDENERS

Sometimes in this war we fight each other. Scarcity of land and varying interpretations of what is neglected space mean that one guerrilla group may dig up another's garden and plant their own. Two of my large concrete tubs suffered this fate. Both were marginal patches, and after they were first vandalized I changed my planting

* The street names somewhat ironically translate as 'sorrow' and 'arduous' streets.

to make them less flamboyant and provocative to the offenders. Both schemes were dug up again. This time, my flatmate Meike 155 spotted Joe 601 from over the road replacing my nasturtiums (*Tropaeolum majus* 'Tom Thumb') with a flowering forsythia (*Forsythia* x *intermedia*), and in the tub where I had put violets (*Viola canina*) my new next-door neighbour Silvano 2042 stuck in a huge bamboo tree (*Phyllostachys aurea*). I found out later that neither of them knew I had been gardening in these locations, but on hearing about guerrilla gardening had come to the conclusion that the neglected planters near them could be improved. My initial irritation soon turned into delight as both their plants flourished far better than mine had, and their interest encouraged me to raise my standards elsewhere.

This example makes light of a serious issue. If we are gardening land illicitly, surely someone else has equal right to do so, especially if your use is excluding them and they think they can make better use of the patch?

Inevitably sometimes guerrilla gardeners' squabbles turn into serious battles. Perhaps the most devastating example comes from just south of Santo Antônio in Brazil. Fifteen families had occupied some unused land for over a decade, but the owners of a nearby cattle ranch wanted to expand in their direction. Neither had any more of a legal claim to the land than the other. In August 1981 the cattle ranchers hired eighteen thugs to do their dirty work, offering them half the land if they evicted the 'squatters'. They tied everyone up, burned their huts, destroyed stocks of food and crops, sent possessions that could not be burned floating down the river and dropped off the peasants beside a distant stretch of highway. But the families returned to their land, rebuilt their huts and salvaged their crops. When the thugs returned, the peasants drove them off with gunfire. Fortunately the Brazilian land reform agency intervened, and by 1983 the peasants had title to the land.

6.7 Comfort Missions

Mao specifies that in every company of 122 guerrillas there should be ten cooks (and a barber). By that ratio we should have one cook for every twelve guerrilla gardeners (and perhaps a barber's right arm). Twelve guerrilla gardeners is a fairly typical contingent for digs. Mao describes the cooks' contribution as a 'comfort mission' and recommends serving 'tea and rice'. I have yet to enjoy rice while out gardening, but self-appointed 'cooks' have brought all sorts of tasty snacks for energy, warmth and friendliness.

On their first digs, Sarah 288 provided home-made Anzac biscuits, Lyla 1046 brought a flask of hot chocolate, Tom 354 shared his wife's chocolate brownies and Veronika 1437 came with a picnic of hummus, cheese and biscuits. Stiffer stuff works for some – Jim 006 maintains his spirits with a hip-flask of whisky – and hitting the pub before closing time is a good incentive to keep up the pace (a pub is also a handy place to wash off the street dirt).

One of the most heart-warming occurrences on any dig is a stranger arriving with a tray of steaming mugs and biscuits. This gesture is a sure sign that the local community is being won round. They know what you are doing, they like it, they want to help and they want to introduce themselves. There is no more welcome way to do so: tea tastes best when it is from a stranger, late at night, on a roadside, after a couple of hours' gardening.

Yes, it happens. While I was digging on a traffic island near Blackfriars Bridge in London, a security guard called Sikander came over from a nearby office and took requests for fresh fruit juice and bananas. I have even been sent a cheque by a well-wisher, who insisted that we spent it on a slap-up meal. Enjoy the refreshments and then gently remind those supplying them that the plants too will welcome even more regular drinks, should they have time to water them.

7. PROPAGANDA

'You walk down the block and you can smell it,' said one gardener to me, proudly taking a drag on Manhattan air as he strode towards the Clinton Community Garden. Like a bakery, with its smell of fresh bread wafting out, a fragrant garden sells itself. Aided by the birds and bees it attracts, the garden self-propagates, spreading its seed far and wide. This natural propaganda* hits the senses of passers-by too, whether or not they are hungry for nature's nectar. The lure is all the stronger when that powerful floral burst – something like

Our guerrilla gardening makes front-page news of the local newspaper in Stratford, east London.

---

* *Propaganda* is a word associated with communication, while *propagation is* associated with horticulture, but they are actually closely related. Our use of the word *propaganda* comes from the Latin expression '*propaganda fide*', which means 'propagating the faith'.

mock orange (*Philadelphus coronarius*) or Carolina allspice (*Calycanthus floridus*) – hits you moments after a gust of the more familiar urban street cocktail of diesel fumes, tobacco smoke and dog shit. The smell of a garden can draw you in before you have even seen the flowers. It makes you linger and begin to appreciate the garden more fully. Your heart is won and then your mind.

Adam 276 says the 'ooh and aah factor' is critical for a successful community garden. Guerrilla gardens that set out to be horticulturally spectacular will unavoidably make a powerful statement to all who see (or smell) them. This statement is a positive declaration of victory, of the garden's and gardener's success.

Do not imagine, however, that the natural scent and colour of a garden are enough in themselves to ensure victory. You need to boost the garden's natural propaganda with some man-made intervention. A successful baker does not sell bread by its smell and golden appearance alone.

Propaganda is essential if your activity is to be anything more than a leisurely skirmish. Hans von Dach, in his guide to guerrilla warfare, states: 'The population is your greatest friend. Without their sympathy and active support you will be unable to exist for extended periods of time.'* The same is true of your garden. Propaganda is a key way of winning their sympathy. Che, who devotes several pages to this subject, sums it up thus: 'The revolutionary idea should be diffused by means of appropriate media to the greatest depth possible.'

Do not be intimidated by this need. Propaganda need not be about mind-bending subliminal messages – although flower power hero John Lennon did admit in his song of the same name that

* Hans von Dach was a Swiss army major who wrote a guerrilla warfare manual in 1958, when there was a widespread anxiety that Switzerland would need to prepare to resist an invading aggressor or occupation. The manual was used by civilians to become effective guerrillas. In the absence of imminent invasion, I encourage gardening instead.

'mind games' and planting seeds can go together: 'We're playing those mind games together, pushing the barriers, planting seeds, playing the mind guerrilla.'* Propaganda is not about trickery; it is simply about spreading a straightforward message effectively.

Propaganda serves two main aims: recruitment and protection.

Recruitment:

— Attracting new troops to help you dig or make donations.

— Encouraging others to be guerrilla gardeners in the area.

Protection:

— Ensuring the public enjoys the garden, so that you have support should it be threatened.

— Deterring damage by letting people know volunteers cultivated it.

With these twin purposes in mind we will now consider a broad range of propaganda techniques that I have experimented with and learnt from other guerrilla gardeners. Propaganda is an unpredictable tool, so although the following pages might appear to be a neat prescription for creating a positive impact in your area they do not guarantee it. Putting a message out there really is like planting a seed: you cannot be sure whether it will flourish or wither, whether it will turn into the beautiful specimen pictured on the packet or an alarmingly rampant nuisance smothering everything else you are trying to achieve. I see there being seven pillars to propaganda. Which you use will depend on how ambitious you are for your garden, and the strength of your sense of purpose.

---

* 'Mind Games' was the title track of an album released in November 1973. It was recorded in New York City during the summer of 1973, which is precisely when Liz Christy and the Green Guerillas began to transform the Bowery-Houston area of the city. Perhaps Lennon picked up on news of the guerrilla gardeners when writing the lyrics.

7.1 Conversation

Although our activity is illegal, discreet and often carried out under the cover of darkness, we do not need to feel like spies in the night. We certainly do not need to deceive our loved ones with elaborate excuses for why we come home with mud all over our hands and knees.

So, the first place to start your propaganda mission is at home. Gain the trust and perhaps even the enthusiasm of your next of kin, friends and family. This is essential. While your ultimate aim should be to recruit them to fight alongside you, there are other more pressing concerns that make it essential to tell them about your activity at the earliest stage. These are the people to whom you will turn should anything untoward happen in the field – an arrest, perhaps, or an accident. Do not wait until after something has gone horribly wrong to explain to them what you were doing. I do not mean to worry you – guerrilla gardening is relatively safe – but think of basic propaganda as common-sense safety. Imagine your family at your funeral, agonizing about why you were found dead on a roundabout with a fork and a tray of pansies. Propaganda need go no further than telling them what you are doing.

Tell someone before your trowel has even cut the soil. This public promise will be propaganda that gives you the impetus to get gardening. Talk about the end result, the fun of gardening, treat any of the risks lightly (you should by now have been reassured that these are low anyway) and describe the success of others, using this as evidence that you will be successful as well. You will know which of your friends are likely to be most receptive or sceptical.

I first turned to friends when I decided to attack a larger territory than I could tackle on my own. I recruited two who were obviously enthusiastic gardeners – Lizzie 002, who had just begun an evening class in gardening, and Andrew 003, who was so keen to garden that he had volunteered to spend weekends weeding the driveway of his marketing clients. These two were easy converts, but lived too far away to be anything more than an occasional force. I next turned to two local friends who had no previous experience of gardening. The subject was raised at the end of a boozy meal in my flat. With everyone already in good spirits the situation rapidly escalated from being an amusing anecdote to immediate action. Despite the chilly autumn weather Joe 004 and Clara 005 joined me that night to plant herbs on a traffic island. This was no drunken one-night stand, as three years later they are still among the regular troops.

Unless you garden in the dead of night in the middle of nowhere, you are likely to be doing so as members of the public pass by. Do not fear them. Every single one is a potential conscript. Get comfortable with seeing part of your mission as letting them know what you are doing. Most will walk past, oblivious to you or perhaps a little scared, but there are plenty of curious folk out there who are keen to talk with you while you garden in public. If you are taking a cautious, unassuming approach (disguised as a municipal worker, for example) conversation may be limited to just the local busybodies. This influential crowd are confident about approaching official-looking people and challenging anyone in the area who is doing something they have not been told about. They will ask, 'Who asked you to garden?' and 'Who is funding it?' Tell them the truth – it usually wins them round – and they will spread the word. You can make yourself more likely to be approached by turning up in greater numbers, waving a video camera around, making abundant biscuits obviously available, and encouraging the troops to take a break from their digging and catch the eye of strangers. Bring along spare tools and give them something to do. All of this is not what is expected from gardeners in public space and will ensure you are noticed, but you will need to be prepared to deal with interest from pests too.

Conversation may not occur the first time you garden, but it is more likely to do so as time goes by. Both your presence and your motives will become more visible. On subsequent visits strangers may appear bearing gifts of tea or offering the use of their bathroom. I have had drivers spot me, pull over to the kerb and thrust money into my muddy gloves when they recognize what we are doing. The first time this happened there was a moment of ambiguity about what service was expected from me, but there was no negotiation – they expected nothing but to drive past flowers.

Once you have positively blooming results to show, or even guerrilla-grown produce to serve your friends, it becomes all the easier to win support. If you have a large guerrilla garden that can be enjoyed for leisurely recreation, then invite passers-by in – it is their garden too. Do not let them assume that your garden is private. Take friends on a stroll around your block to see the patches you have dug, point out the poppies flourishing on a railway embankment that you seed-bombed on the way to work, show them dramatic 'before and after' pictures. You never know what you might plant in their minds.

My Mother 008 was taking my Aunt Clare on a little tour around her locality in Plymouth to show off her guerrilla garden when coincidence intervened and the most important man in the city appeared on the pavement – the Lord Mayor of Plymouth. This was an opportunity for decisive conversation. My provocative Aunt Clare challenged him with the incongruity between the beautiful scene and its criminal origin. 'There's been some illegal activity here. You know there's been some guerrilla gardening?' He apparently reviewed the scene, smiled and said, 'It all looks very pleasant to me.' Common sense prevailed, of course, and as a result my Mother has acquired the 'support of the Mayor' should she ever face aggro from officials. It is in this casual, opportunistic manner that guerrilla gardening battles are won and guerrilla gardens are legitimized.

7.2 Leaflets and Pamphlets

A determined guerrilla should not simply rely on local passers-by to take an interest. Some sites are not near busy thoroughfares; your dig will not necessarily coincide with the flurry of commuters coming home, or closing time at the local pub. To ensure more heartfelt appreciation you will need to ensure your actions are not credited to the local authority gardeners after you have gone.

One basic way is to bring leaflets. Print out notes explaining who you are and what you are doing. Keep them in a pocket to hand to the curious, or go for blanket coverage and appoint someone to be an official distributor of leaflets, thrusting them at passers-by in the same determined fashion as those who promote club nights and discount hair salons. Localize the contents by making a specific reference to the place where you are gardening. Invite people to offer support by joining in, making a donation or just keeping an eye on the patch and informing you if it needs maintenance. Direct them to a website or your contact details. This is straightforward political propaganda adapted to your cause. Keep it simple and keep it fun. Conversation is more personal and more likely to win someone over, but you can reach more people more quickly with leaflets.

The guerrilla gardeners of the Toronto Public Space Committee have produced a beautiful and informative pamphlet that they distribute when out fighting neglect. I have printed A4 posters on bright green paper and decorate street furniture with them – inside a phone box, on a bus stop, round a litterbin. These delicate sheets do not last as long as flowers, but for a while they spread the word. Try asking in local shops and bars; some will be happy to display a poster in their window, proud to be associated with an initiative of community improvement. Take this opportunity to brief them about what you have been doing so that they can become surrogate mouthpieces.

No Dogs
Except Guide dogs

M
AV

Back the Bid

LONDON
2012
CANDIDATE CITY

at london2012.com

GUERRILLA
GARDENING
AT VICARAGE LANE, STRATFORD

IN MAY 2006 & AGAIN IN OCTOBER A RAISED FLOWER BED ON VICARAGE LANE HAS
BEEN WEEDED, GRAVELLED AND PLANTED WITH EXOTIC GRASSES, SHRUBS AND BULBS.
THIS HAS BEEN VOLUNTARY WORK BY THE GUERRILLA GARDENERS COSTING OVER £30.
IT IS YOUR SPACE, YOURS TO ENJOY, AND YOURS TO CARE FOR.
THANKS.
www.GuerrillaGardening.org

Ki
R
The No.1 Cho
New The

chicke
In UK

Another approach is a letter addressed to local residents. This is particularly appropriate if a patch of land has a logical geographic link with certain buildings and could be seen as more their land than yours. Five of us in London gardened a planter that ran along a wall in front of a small tower block called Charles Allen House. None of us lived there and we had only met one shy resident on the first evening's dig, so the next time we visited I left twenty letters in their lobby explaining that we had filled their wall with hardy cyclamen (*Cyclamen hederifolium*) and sweet peas (*Lathyrus odoratus*). It asked to them to consider occasionally watering and weeding the wall – and it worked. Several weeks later I found the flowers thriving, and several appreciative residents gave us ice cream and began quizzing us for help about how to improve other areas around their tower.

A local newsagent was happy to display a poster for us that declared our recent guerrilla gardening in Vicarage Lane, east London.

You can go even further. Give people something to chew over. This book is propaganda. Mao and Che wrote books too, and the original guerrilla gardener was a prolific pamphleteer. In 1648, before he had even begun guerrilla gardening, Gerrard Winstanley wrote five pamphlets covering many subjects, including the desire to cultivate neglected common land for the benefit of the poor and hungry.

Actually Winstanley's experience is a useful lesson: do not get carried away with the writing and forget that your garden itself is propaganda. Winstanley wrote many pamphlets when he should have been getting on with transforming St George's Hill into a vegetable garden; the majority of the population – those who he wanted to join him – were still illiterate in seventeenth-century England. More unfortunate still was the stridency of his writing. The authorities had greater fear of the implications of his grand vision than of the guerrilla gardening itself, and their repressive response scuppered his campaign within eighteen months. He has left an inspiring written legacy* but

* In 1918 Gerrard Winstanley was one of nineteen 'thinkers and fighters' to have their name engraved on a granite obelisk in Moscow's Aleksandrovsky Garden. It was erected at Lenin's request to celebrate the first anniversary of the Bolshevik revolution.

retired unfulfilled. Do not let propaganda upstage your gardening. Your words will have more impact alongside visibly healthy plants. Remember these essential principles:

— Focus your message on the battle of horticultural opportunity rather than wrapping it up with complaints or other ambitions.
— Play down the long-term implications of what you are doing, at least initially. While you may feel you are starting a revolution, try not to let the authorities know this.
— Ensure your message is getting to the people you need to help you in the garden, not just to landowners and lawyers.

7.3 Signs

The Toronto Public Space Committee encourages people to water their *Tagetes patula* in Nassau Street.

The urge to stick a stake in the ground and mark the garden as your achievement is the same one that motivated Aldrin and Armstrong to stick the Stars and Stripes into the moon. You are saying, 'I was here, I did this' – and, to some extent, 'This is mine'. You are bursting with pride about how amazing it looks. You and your troops not only want the credit but also know that passers-by would probably appreciate the garden more if they knew how it had come about. It is not just another private garden or tax-funded municipal planting scheme. You want to encourage them to take care of it, water the plants and clear the litter: in other words, to share in the space. Signage seems the obvious answer. It is what we are used to in public places. There are a few things to consider, however, before going out there and making your mark.

My first labelling was much like a regular gardener's. I stuck in little wooden stakes on which I wrote 'Gardened by guerrillas', but they were virtually invisible and easily pinched. In Toronto, Erin 158 and her guerrilla gardeners in the Kensington area have pasted

messages and pictures on to T-shaped posts, inviting passers-by to water the plants, and informing them that guerrilla gardeners were responsible. They keep the message simple, a few words easily digested. In Berlin, Julia 013 has hung similar notices and promoted her related website on wooden boards strung from the tree. Their deliberately home-made look and cheerful messages are a charming antidote to corporate notices. But they are vulnerable to the elements, and like a showy annual require replanting each season.

Spray-painting a stencil would give you a clearer sign for longer, but it is likely to be eradicated by street cleaners – even the entertaining and popular graffiti of Banksy is cleaned up fairly quickly by the European cities in which he leaves his mark. One greener and more virtuous alternative to oil-based spray paints is 'clean graffiti'. A mark is left by sand-blasting, jet-spraying or scrubbing a wall hard with a shoe brush through a stencil, cleaning off the urban grime to leave your message as a bright, fresh surface. You could call this partial or selective cleaning. In Leeds, a graffiti artist (though not a guerrilla gardener) called Moose has been doing this, but bizarrely was ordered to 'clean up' by the local council.

'Moss graffiti' is another nice, environmentally friendly-sounding idea. Andrea 738 in Vancouver (a blogger at HeavyPetal.ca) has a recipe for moss graffiti: blend a milkshake-like combination of two cups of creamy milk, a can of beer or water and a handful of living moss. You just paint this on to a stone surface wherever you want the moss to grow, keep it fairly damp and watch it flourish. Or plant messages with flowers: Andrew 1679 has sown nasturtiums (*Tropaeolum majus* 'Empress of India') in Hackney, London, spelling 'GG' for guerrilla gardening.

I have been offered more visible and permanent signage by generous benefactors – even a big round green plaque with our logo on it just like the blue plaques that the British put on buildings where historic figures once lived. I did not take up the offer. For modest plots and casual roadside ones this would be too heavy-handed, and it strays into the realms of commercial advertising. For most of us, guerrilla gardening is about making our environment visually attractive with flowers, not cluttering it with signage. There are plenty of hoardings in cities already.

The ugliness of signage in gardens is clear to see in places where councils have invited local businesses to fund public gardening in exchange for advertising space. A bold notice is erected among the flowers (or quite often in a miserable expanse of badly maintained grass) that season after season tells a bad pun or reminds one of a revolting restaurant. The worst I have seen is on a slip road of the M40 motorway and advertises a brand of beds. Plants and hedging are arranged into four giant flowerbeds in the shape of double beds and labelled 'Dreams Roundabout – Beds by Dreams'. You may laugh (I did when I first saw it), but really the gag would have been funnier without being spelled out day after day.

Permanent signage is most appropriate if you are creating a community garden. The sign then marks the space as something different from ordinary municipal land and can convey information such as opening hours, garden rules and how to become a community gardener. The Liz Christy gardeners include a short history of the garden on their gate. The Clinton Community Garden has a notice that greets the passer-by in English, Spanish and Arabic. Elsewhere, notices explain fundraising initiatives and point out donation boxes, tool sheds and native planting schemes.

In a mature community garden, signage becomes another symbol of the spirit of the place, as with any community space, be it a pub, a gym or a church. For guerrilla gardeners who go legal, a sign is the clearest stamp of approval. Margaret 2878 has a metal plaque on the churchyard wall commending her garden for being 'Outstanding' in the 2007 Britain in Bloom Neighbourhood Awards.

Since 2002 big round green plastic plaques have been tied to the fences of community gardens across New York. On each one is the maple-leaf insignia of the New York City Department of Parks and Recreation, marking them out as publicly owned protected spaces.

7.4 Events

We celebrated Christmas (and the flourishing of this guerrilla garden) by decorating our *Picea abies* on St George's Circus, London.

Beyond the publicity of a guerrilla gardening event – street theatre to some – there are two other types of event a guerrilla gardener should consider organizing to win over hearts and minds.

The first is preparatory training exercises. These sessions are an opportunity to galvanize your force, outline your objectives, discuss tactics and weed out troops who may not be fit for duty. They can happen away from the front line. Oren 2359 in Vancouver has organized a series of training sessions for his new group. At these, recruits pay $5 and in return receive a tutorial and some food. Their message board is currently enlisting locals for a serious-sounding session that 'lays out the basis of soil components and their functions – bacteria, fungi, and carbon-nitrogen ratios'. Ava 949 in San Diego, California, invited round her friends to make seed bombs. I had a Christmas tree decorations-making evening in my flat at which six of us spent the evening piercing dried sliced oranges with string and eating mince pies.

The other kind of event that can have an extremely powerful propaganda effect is the garden party. Such an event can be difficult and unpleasant to stage on a small roadside verge, but if possible find a way to have a barbecue in or near your garden. Be grateful for the opportunity to eat good food in beautiful surroundings and share it with as many people as you can, potential guerrilla gardeners from far and wide. It should be a public party.

Many community gardens have summer barbecues and other sociable inclusive activities. The guerrilla gardeners of the Rosa Rose Garden in Berlin have painted a large white panel on the wall of a neighbouring building on to which they project films for community screenings. Fireworks, fêtes and films were hosted by Parisian guerrilla gardeners in Le Jardin Solidaire. Crystal 965 of New York's Lower East Side wrote a musical about the creation of that city's community gardens for performance in such a garden. I picked up a poster from the 6th and B Garden in New York's East Village that listed events ranging from yoga classes and a performance by a blues-based jazz trio to readings from a book about the aftermath of the 9/11 attacks and a film about the Baader-Mainhof gang – all occurring within one month!

An event does not even need to happen in your garden. In New York, Ellen 686 organized a bike ride to rally people into potential guerrilla action by taking them past five different community gardens that were threatened with destruction. In San Francisco, Brian 1525 has also led supporters of guerrilla gardening on bike rides from garden to garden to encourage them to get more involved.

7.5 Competitions

Competition has encouraged spectacular tree pit planting on the streets of Berlin. This one is in Oranienburger Strasse.

Conflict of all sorts generates publicity. Add a new front to your war by entering the fray of garden competitions. Who has the most beautiful garden, the biggest vegetables, the most successful seed bomb design? It spurs you on, creates some news, and can even be a way of protecting your garden through a degree of legitimization. Liz Christy and the Green Guerillas won the Mollie Parnis Dress Up Your Neighborhood Award in the second year of her guerrilla gardening.

Donald 277 tells me the community gardens in New York's East Village still compete from time to time. It is perhaps a sign of maturity

that as the conflict with authorities and developers waned, so the retired guerrillas needed to find the excitement of battle elsewhere. In Berlin, the enthusiasm for guerrilla gardening tree pits was harnessed when BUND, the local official open spaces organization, legitimized it and turned it into a competition. The result has been a varied explosion of colour along the streets as gardeners take on a tree or two each and try to out-wow their neighbours.

I have entered two guerrilla gardens in competitions, both of which required no effort beyond my regular gardening but provided a degree of entertainment. My first tentative gesture towards legitimacy was to enter a civic gardening competition. Greening Southwark offered awards for private front gardens, schools, hospitals and shops. My entry was none of these, but I wondered if this mattered anyway, since my gardening was still in the spirit of the tournament. All you had to do was complete an entry form, after which a judge secretly inspected the garden and decided whether you were prize-worthy.

I entered the 'front garden' category, although 'my' front garden was not only *their* garden and *their* responsibility but also about twenty metres beneath my sixth-floor flat. I was sure they would notice, but decided that coming clean about my guerrilla gardening in the context of a horticultural competition would make it more likely that the authorities would give my activities the nod. But the judge came and went and I received an invitation to the awards ceremony with no comment about my eligibility, or lack of it.

I had mixed feelings about the response. Did they really consider the space to be my front garden, or was their judging so sloppy that they did not notice the peculiarity? Whatever the reason,* I gained a certificate of commendation for the 'Front garden of 39 Perronet

* Two years later when I approached the council again I discovered the judging was just laissez-faire and Southwark council did not for one moment assume the space was my front garden.

House' and it was to become my 'get out of jail free' card should anyone at the council prove difficult in the future.

The other competition I entered quite openly as a guerrilla gardener. I was encouraged by CSV, the UK's largest volunteering and training organization, to take part in their annual Make a Difference Day by arranging a dig. Earlier that year I had met their Executive Director, Dame Elizabeth 064, who, with a twinkle in her eye, had thoroughly encouraged what we were up to. So on a chilly evening in October 2006, eleven of us led by Tim 035 transformed a raised roadside planter in New Cross, south London, while simultaneously all sorts of other voluntary activity was taking place across the country. The events were all judged, and the lucky ones were to be invited to a glittering champagne dinner and awarded funding.

A few weeks later I received a congratulatory letter inviting Tim and me to the event and announcing our short-listing for the Ground Breaking Achievement Award (a particularly appropriate title even though the category was not specifically linked to breaking ground). In due course I attended the bash at the palatial Plaisterers' Hall in the City of London. Once again, sadly, guerrilla gardening missed out on the top award, losing to 100 Scots who had spent the day cleaning dog mess from the parks of Govan.

Whether you start your own or enter someone else's, I highly recommend you take part in competitions. I cope with my repeated failure in them by knowing that everyone is a winner.

7.6 Media

The media offer the most powerful propaganda tool for the guerrilla gardener. They can spread the message far and wide, and say things that you cannot convey with flowers. The truly ambitious guerrilla gardener should learn to use all kinds of media.

I recommend you first create your own media outlet online. You are in control of this. Plant a virtual garden, show pictures of what you have done or a short film, announce forthcoming events, outline your objectives, provide contact details. People from all over the world can pay a visit to your webgarden – it is, after all, just another dimension of public space, but one that is even more accessible and can look beautiful all year round. Luc 158 uploads hundreds of pictures of his street-side project in Montreal to a Flickr photo album. Girasol 829 uses Blogger (Brussels-Farmer.blogspot.com) to display pictures of his sunflowers, as well as a manifesto, links to other sites and media clips. Anon 946 in Australia uses MySpace (MySpace.com/Guerrilla_Gardening) to display pictures of his vegetable patch on a roundabout and a 'Manifesto of the Guerrilla Gardening Sydney Chapter' while simultaneously blasting visitors with Guns and Roses' 'Welcome to the Jungle'. Facebook seems particularly popular with Canadian guerrilla gardeners, and several groups have sprouted there. David 2384 built his own colourful website (GuerillaGardeners.wn6.co.uk) from scratch to attract support in the rural community of Standish, Lancashire. Julia 013 built her website to appeal well beyond her local community, so although she is based in Berlin her website (GrueneWelle.org) is available in German, English and Spanish.

Visitors to your site are likely to be supportive, because they will have heard about it from another website or a friend, or because they had the curiosity to seek you out. Whatever online approach you choose, if you want widespread impact, a website is recommended.

It is through your website that the broadcast media are most likely to come across your garden. For news desks our story is a rare bit of good news. Fashion magazines, property pages and even motoring magazines have all found an angle about guerrilla gardening that is right for them and (so far) have covered the story positively; gardening magazines occasionally take an interest too.

Soliciting the media need not take much of your time. They are most likely to come to you, having heard on the grapevine that something is up in your area, but call them if necessary. Local newspapers are a good place to start seeding your story, because it is directly relevant to their readers. Donald 277 has been using the media to help him guerrilla-garden in New York for 35 years. When I asked him if there was ever a time when he turned down a request he shook his head vigorously. 'You always say yes to the press. It can't hurt.'

There was in fact one time when he had some trouble, but the piece never made it to print. He let a photographer and crew from a fashion magazine into the Liz Christy Community Garden. 'They brought this woman in and all of a sudden the top of her dress comes off.' He had to put a swift stop to the guerrilla pornography shoot. 'We don't mind fashion shoots here,' he said, 'but it doesn't look good if someone is topless in the garden.'

The fact that you see yourself as a guerrilla gardener does not mean you must always hide. If you use the media well they become a mouthpiece. Some in our ranks despise the media for being a manipulative, exploitative distraction in society and stay well clear of enquiries. This is short-sighted. Even Che, an imperialist-hating communist radical, appeared on American TV, not as a shadowy guerrilla figure in a jungle, but in a studio discussion on CBS's *Face the Nation* as head of the Cuban delegation to the United Nations.

When a journalist calls, answer their questions in as matter-of-fact a way as you can. It is important that you avoid the risk of playing up to media stereotypes. Generally, people who do something illegal, particularly if it is at night, are shifty and reluctant to talk about it – eccentric at best, obstructive at worst. On the other hand, people who spend lots of their time doing community work have a reputation for being a bit dull, which makes neither a good story nor appealing propaganda. The journalist may well have a preconceived idea that you are a naive eccentric fool and be looking to play this up. Your role is to convey that you are anything but this – just an enthusiastic average gardener who is keen to take responsibility for public space and who sees the illegality of the activity as a silly quirk of the world we live in.

Emphasize that guerrilla gardeners include all kinds of people doing all sorts of different things. Perhaps you are more into growing vegetables, passionate about native plants or working towards making a large community garden for local children. Talk that up, but remind them of the breadth and popularity of the activity. Giving them a sense of guerrilla gardening's normality will both protect your reputation and make the activity more appealing to those who are hearing about it for the first time.

Meet the journalist and get someone with a camera there too. You want to share the beauty of your garden, so if you do a radio interview make sure you have a way of directing listeners to some pictures (requesting a plug for your website is logical). Taking a journalist into the field with you really helps. It is only after an evening's dig with us, journalists have admitted to me, that they have understood the appeal of our activity. The result has invariably been a more eulogistic report. Let them know when you are next planning to go gardening and invite them to join you. Let them see that you are a gardener of action. Remember what you want to say, steer the conversation that way and get them involved and complicit – Kelvin 363 from the *South China Morning Post* set a fine example when he stayed digging for hours with me after everyone else had gone home.

Afterwards, they might call up the authorities to ask for a comment. Let them – the authorities will have little to say in response to this awkward confrontation. All of this is good for you and the garden. Before they have even published a word, they are spreading news around, attracting people to the cause and creating a buffer of good publicity that the powers that be will struggle to challenge. Keep a photographic record of your gardening – 'before and after' photos are a great way to win support.

The media will tend to exaggerate the scale of your support, the scale of your garden and the delight of local residents. The thousands of people on my database have been reported in some media as thousands of people actively guerrilla gardening. On the face of it that is all great. It celebrates your achievement and it helps normalize the activity, making our battle less intimidating and peculiar for those who want to strike out and do their first dig. But it can also get in the way. Media myth can overtake the reality of your deeds and create expectations that are hard to match. Publicity creates troops eager for leadership and advice, supportive followers looking for instruction. You may have too many beating a path to your inbox to know what to do with them all. It is rare, but it happens. I had 50 new volunteers turn up to one small dig in Stratford and it was chaos because we just did not have enough gardening for everyone to do. The media may also exaggerate the extent of your resources, prompting a flurry of calls from those living in areas suffering from horticultural blight, thinking you are there to help.

Guerrillas risk being distorted into mythological characters. The story of Che Guevara is a warning from history for all of us. His reputation is almost entirely founded on that iconic photo by Alberto Korda rather than his record as a guerrilla – other than in his role alongside Fidel Castro in the Cuban Revolution of 1959, Che was not a success. Yet he is the popular global embodiment of the revolutionary guerrilla spirit. The media have given the public the image of a man they wanted to believe in, but it has not done much for Che's cause. The same is sometimes true for us 'horticultural heroes'. Keep the media and your reputation in check or else your propaganda will overtake your achievements.*

* Despite media reports I am not the founder or father of guerrilla gardening – it is a flattering but false allegation.

7.7 Merchandise

A healthy garden is a productive space, spewing forth flowers, seedlings and crops of fruit and vegetables. It is screaming out to the rest of nature to be noticed, and usually offers something in return. A flower's sweet nectar, a satisfying seed and a juicy tomato are a garden's way of attracting the birds and bees and propagating the plants. Canny guerrilla gardeners help their plants along and sell or exchange their crop, giving them the opportunity to invest in new plants and materials. Christopher 1594 sells pistol-shaped seed bombs online for $75 (ThreeMiles.com). In London we raised funds by harvesting the flowers of our 200 lavender bushes and selling them dried and stuffed into bright red pillows. Julia 013 auctioned amaranth (*Amaranthus hypochondriacus*) seeds at a Berlin guerrilla garden party. The potential for a profit is there, with overheads so low. (The land certainly comes cheap.)

My living room becomes a drying room for the harvest of aromatic *Lavandula angustifolia*.

More importantly, the transaction also spreads the word about how successful your garden is. It is evidence not only that you have gone out and planted something as a guerrilla gardener but that it has survived so well as to flourish into a productive crop. With your harvest for sale you have the chance to bring the guerrilla gardening message to a much broader group of sympathetic supporters, because it will connect you with those people who are not specifically interested in gardening. As they take the brown paper bag full of produce, relate the tale of your struggle to grow it all and the miracle of making productive land out of waste ground. If you tell it well, they will probably pass the story on.

As you plant your guerrilla garden, consider what is likely to be a good crop for propaganda purposes. Vegetables are hard work and you will probably eat all that you grow. Guerrilla gardening merchandise tends to involve crops that are easy to grow and are so abundant that you have far too much to keep. Start simply by collecting the pea-sized seeds that drop off nasturtiums (*Tropaeolum majus*) at the end of summer, or shaking out a handful of the fine dusty black seeds from a poppy (*Papaver rhoeas*) into an envelope. Chappers 046 gives away wildflower seeds in Cornwall, and the Brussels Farmers distributed sunflower seeds (*Helianthus annuus*) in a branded paper envelope.

Another way to achieve propaganda is to lend your support to someone else's merchandise and thereby piggyback on their investment in promoting the message. 'Sell out!' I hear you cry. I agree. Marrying your ambitions with someone else's commercial objectives is an extremely high-risk strategy. We can learn a lesson from the sorry story of some guerrilla gardeners in Brussels who decided to join up with a major auto conglomerate for the launch of their little city car. This was not a smart idea. Over a beer Girasol 829 related the unfortunate tale to me.

The marque's advertising agency were scouring the web for 'European urban heroes' and found the guerrilla gardeners. They proposed making a short film about them, which would be shown on the car's website, along with a profile of the group. The agency agreed to give the guerrillas a weblink, publish the key points of their manifesto and feature the presentation of a gift of sunflower seeds within the film. Girasol 829 was uncomfortable and walked away at this point, but the others continued.

Things began to go wrong on the shoot. The film-makers wanted to show the finished results of planting sunflower seeds – not easy on a one-day shoot in spring. Their solution was to use a plastic sunflower, and they reassured the guerrillas that, thanks to the magic of television, this would be indistinguishable from a real sunflower. Foolishly the guerrillas agreed. Weeks later the website went live and the plastic plant became an obvious joke. Nor was this the only stitch-up, because there was no sign of any of the other agreed points. The promised one million extra visitors to the guerrillas' website never came. They complained, and a fortnight later the car company added a link, but it was too little, too late. They gained nothing from this propaganda exercise and arguably lost some goodwill and confidence.

The same manufacturer's UK ad agency contacted me too about a partnership with GuerrillaGardening.org. The caller told me how keen they were to promote the new petrol car's ecological credentials in the battle against electric vehicles, and that our independent approach to community environmental improvement was just what they liked. His honesty made it easy for me to turn them down.

There is an adage that all publicity is good publicity. I do not agree; bad publicity can be terrible. On the other hand, there is a popular assumption that all propaganda is bad propaganda; I do not agree with that either. Use it well, and sow gardens far and wide.

8. VICTORY

This is a win-win war. Take a public place of wasted opportunity and turn it into a garden. In time victory should be clear to everyone, and probably fragrant too.

Luc 158 and his award-winning guerrilla garden on the pavement of Sherbrooke East, Montreal.

But identifying the moment of victory is not easy. The challenge of fighting scarcity and neglect on a global scale seems distant and insurmountable as you dig away trying to transform a tatty tree pit. Even if you bring the challenge down in size, your triumphant garden does not stand beautifully to attention for long. Battles are not predictable as exciting new opportunities and disappointing diversions blow you off course. Savouring a garden and declaring peace is not a simple matter for the enthusiast – after all, most gardeners enjoy the ongoing tussle with nature.

For any kind of guerrilla the fight is more vaguely defined than for someone in a conventional confrontation, and so the guerrilla gardener must accept that victory is not clear-cut. It comes in many shades of green so, like a botanist scrutinizing a plant specimen, let us try to identify what victory can be.

8.1 Little Victory

The first step is making the most of any triumph. Look for little victories. Guerrilla gardening is itself a global movement working towards lots of little victories. It is not a monolithic campaign fighting for one big universal outcome, but instead seeks countless independent local initiatives. By all means think big, but savour success on the way there. There will be plenty of reasons for you to celebrate. Little victories come quickly, and spur you onwards.

Enjoy your plants. Lyla 1046 savours triumph every day as she walks past her sunflower seedlings (*Helianthus annuus*) sprouting in a planter on a north London industrial estate. A trouble-free dig mining a grassy verge with daffodil bulbs (*Narcissus* 'Yellow Cheerfulness') will set you up for several months of satisfaction as you wait for them to explode with colour. Seeing your plants reach maturity in a showy climax of blooms is definitely a victory, even though nature will curtail it in time. Saving and securing the seeds from your plants for future campaigns is a victory – Ground Hog 1698 in Amsterdam showed me her spoils of war, an enormous glass bowl of hollyhock seeds (*Alcea rosea*). Though the seed marks the end of one successful offensive, it holds promise for a new one on an even greater scale.

Enjoy positive reactions: the smile of an appreciative passer-by, the supportive beep of a car's horn, the declarations of thanks. Put 'changing people's perceptions of their community' on your list of

A façade garden of *Viola tricolor* and *Impatiens walleriana* outside a shop in Amsterdam.

little victories; after a resident of Regan Way, Hackney, told me our guerrilla gardening in his area 'would be destroyed by the morning', it was indeed a victory two months later to see his pleasure that the garden was still largely intact. Delight in persuading people to participate. Every conscript you enlist is a little victory. Every passer-by who pours water on the marigolds next to the Toronto guerrilla gardeners' 'Please Water Me' sign is another.

Add your little victories together. Celebrating the first snowdrop sprouting is great, but take a moment a few days later to enjoy the magnificence of a street lined with tree pits full of them. One convert is a victory, but knowing they are out spreading the word is even better. Use these successes as ballast in the storms ahead; think of them as compensation after an act of petty vandalism, or encouragement in the face of apathy from neighbours.

If all goes well you will probably crave greater victories. The triumph of those first flowers may not feel quite as good a few seasons in. You will itch for a new challenge. Respond to this by moving your goalposts, expanding your horizons or embracing whatever cliché about ambition you like. Luc 158 is into his fifth year of planting the huge beds along the sidewalk of Sherbrooke East in Montreal, but the bed is now packed with plants so he is taking his battle to a new front. Success builds confidence, and it has spurred Luc on to a bigger target around the corner.

Share victories by helping someone else guerrilla-garden in their area. The early days of a dig can be the hardest, so your help will be appreciated and you will have another reason to celebrate. My guerrilla gardening spread dig by dig. My territory expanded from the front-door planter of my tower block to the shrubbery beyond, then to the traffic island up the road and onwards to help other Londoners in their areas.

Rome was not built in a day; in fact it took about ten years just to build the Coliseum. Do not expect to make great achievements quickly; when Liz Christy and the Green Guerillas began transforming pockets of New York in the early 1970s, they never dreamed of the huge potential of their actions, nor the enormous impact they would make on the city and beyond. Steve Frillmann of the Green Guerillas described their evolution to me. He explained how modest and simple ambitions at the start – just to make one community garden – made both their garden and others sustainable and popular. Had they started with the grand aspiration of creating hundreds of community gardens, Steve doubts they would have so been successful. Like the Green Guerillas' first garden, your small victory could turn out to be far more impactful than you imagine.

8.2 Legitimization

Guerrilla gardeners do not, by definition, ask permission or seek legitimization from the landowner for what they do. This is for some, if not all, of the following reasons:

— It may never be possible for legitimization to be granted where you want to garden.
— What you are doing is of benefit to everybody anyway and of disadvantage to nobody, so asking permission is unnecessary.
— Permission is more likely to be granted when you have the positive effects of your actions to show the owner, rather than just good intentions.
— Finding the correct person to grant permission is often more trouble than it is worth. They can find you later.

But should gaining legitimacy be right for you, when is the right time and how do you go about getting it?

IT IS NOT ALWAYS NECESSARY

Victory is possible without legitimization. Do not feel that it is an inevitable step. An owner who has neglected a piece of land for years may continue to do so indefinitely. Your intervention may be totally acceptable to that landowner, but not something they wish to be seen sanctioning. So, even though a truce has not been signed, your battle could well be over. Accept that, remembering this: *a guerrilla gardener who wishes to go straight risks losing everything.* You are blowing your cover, you are confessing, you are pointing out your success compared with their failure, you are putting whoever is officially responsible in an embarrassing and defensive position. What you thought was neglect may turn to interference, and what you hoped was a supportive blind eye could become an obstructive beady eye.

Here is a case in point. Freda 850 from High Wycombe, in Buckinghamshire, told me how seeking legitimization turned out to be a terrible mistake for her. As we have heard, she had cleared encroaching ivy (*Hedera helix*) from the public footpath that passed by the bottom of her property and spruced the place up with some new shrubs from her own garden. But this guerrilla gardening nagged Freda's conscience and she decided to seek permission for her colourful landmark. She called the district council, the Land Registry, local solicitors and the Highways Agency, but no one could decide who had the right to give her permission. She persevered in seeking an answer, but was then warned by the district council that she could be prosecuted – for vandalism and obstruction. Eventually the Highways Agency accepted responsibility, by which point Freda had already pre-emptively removed all but the bluebells from her guerrilla garden. She regretted the day she began her enquiries, without which no one would ever have noticed or cared about her intervention.

Sometimes it is absolutely clear-cut that permission will never be granted. Provocative protest-planting attacks in areas that are not neglected – roads, immaculate lawns – are quickly doomed, and cultivating space where the landowner has obstructive rules or alternative plans is just something to enjoy for as long as it goes unnoticed. Marcel 1137, who is 76, has enjoyed his roof garden perched on top of his Prinsengracht flat in Amsterdam for more than a decade. He has never sought permission because he knows his landlord would never grant it.

THE TIME FOR LEGITIMIZATION

The goal of gaining legitimacy is there for the ambitious guerrilla gardener. To achieve a lot usually requires the security that permission gives you. A big garden will be too obvious to go unnoticed, and one in which you want to involve the community will need to be very public. Zachary 922 in New York sums up this step: 'Guerrilla gardening is how you get something started, but community gardening is the follow-through.' That has been the path in his city – less than a year after they began gardening, the Green Guerillas were already in talks with the New York authorities about taking legitimate responsibility for their plots. Despite their initial concern about liability for accidents and worry that the spaces would encourage drinking and loitering, the gardeners' determination and reasonable nature, combined with positive press interest, got them on side.

Ultimately, it was an easy choice for the city. No one else wanted the land, except fly tippers, street workers and rats. The authorities could not look after it as they were broke, and the neglect cost them every time they had to send in the fire department, the sanitation department or a medical examiner to pull out bodies. For the Green Guerillas, legitimization (in the form of short-term leases) gave them greater confidence that their efforts would last and it encouraged them to take on bigger challenges.

Ideally, *you* will choose the time to seek legitimization. Do this when you judge that you and your guerrilla garden will be more at risk if you continue illegally than if you try to go legit. Once you call a truce and offer to negotiate, it is crucial you do this from a strong position. Follow these rules when entering peace talks:

— Show them a clearly attractive space. The more picture-postcard your garden looks, the easier it will be to win support. If your garden design is less obviously showy, be prepared to describe the care you have put into choosing the plants and the improvements you have made to the soil – investments that will not be immediately apparent.
— Provide photographic evidence of its previous horrible state, and back it up with anecdotes about how dangerous and unpopular the area was.
— Prove that you have a long track record of gardening this space, or at least a previous garden. The authorities will be sceptical about the sustainability of your intervention. They are usually pessimistic characters and this scepticism may explain why they have neglected the space themselves.
— Shower them with evidence that you have buckets of support for the garden, particularly if the landowner is a public body. Gather endorsements from the community (particularly the elderly, children and respectable pillars of society), positive media coverage, even evidence that benign wildlife has been attracted there.
— Show that your garden offers benefits that go beyond just making the area more attractive. Does it provide local food? Has it made people feel safer? Are local businesses doing better as a result of it?
— Remember that even if you have a radical political agenda, you must keep this in check until later. The time to evangelize about your alternative vision for society is when you already have a little piece of it secured.

Where once there was filth now *Anemone* x *hybrida* 'Honorine Jobert' and *Crocosmia* x *crocosmiiflora* flower opposite the Department of Health on London Road, Southwark.

Your aim is to make it as difficult as possible for them to say no, and easy for them to say yes. Keep your demands low. You may need help – a better water supply, a fence, clean soil, waste disposal – but for now you just want permission. Only start asking for more once you can see you are winning the argument. I suggest sending one e-mail or letter at a time to one potential authority – the local council, the landowner, local businesses, neighbours. This gives the recipient a chance to mull it over before responding, and avoids the embarrassment of putting them on the spot. They may not have overall authority, but if you get even a vaguely supportive reaction use this when you go to the next potential authority.

Play your cards right and they will offer to help you. They will realize you are presenting them with a win-win situation and become keen to support you; in fact, they may want to share some of the glory of your success. Throughout this, resist the temptation to point out how stupid and lazy they had been before you started guerrilla gardening (I personally find this very difficult) but let your blooming garden do the taunting. Adam 276 sums up the approach: 'They are Caesar; tell them they made the brilliant decision.'

Be careful to get legitimization from the right person. You may think you have permission, only to discover that you need it from someone else. June 715 fell foul of this problem. For eight years June, who is 79, had been tending a traffic island in the idyllic village of Urchfont. She soon had the blessing of her parish council and, as a legitimate gardener of public space, helped them win 'Best Kept Village in Wiltshire 2005'. But one day she was spotted by a highways inspector from the county council who considered her activity dangerous. She was informed that she could garden only if she wore a fluorescent safety jacket and was accompanied by three warning signs and a human lookout. June felt she was the best judge of the risks and was not prepared to drag around huge metal signs or rely on accompaniment. The parish council sympathized with her and she has continued to garden, driven underground (so to speak) by the council's excessive health and safety legislation. 'They can send me to jail if they like,' she declared to a journalist. 'I just want to be left alone to do it.'

The ultimate legitimization comes about if you can find yourself in a position where you are the authority. I have yet to hear of a guerrilla gardener who is a public official responsible for the land, but I have been told about two women in Pittsburgh who began as guerrilla gardeners but then bought four of the lots for themselves.

MY LEGITIMIZATION

Earlier I described how I came to be a guerrilla gardener by tending the neglected beds of Perronet House in London's Elephant & Castle. It is now time to continue my story.

I recently found myself in a position where legitimization was essential for me to continue gardening: Southwark council contractors attacked the guerrilla garden around my tower block home. For more than three years they had not touched it, and I had gradually established an eclectic mix of shrubs, herbaceous perennials and colourful annuals, gaining the gradual interest and support of fellow residents. The council tore into the beds without warning and with savage horticultural ignorance. Gone were all but one of my Swiss chard seedlings (*Beta vulgaris* var. *cicla*), my yellow yarrow (*Achillea* x 'Anthea') and scarlet flax (*Linum grandiflorum*), and worst of all was the slashing of the two-metre-high white butterfly bush (*Buddleia davidii* 'White Profusion') just at the point when it was about to flower. What happened next was a bumpy ride towards legitimization, a process that unearthed scandal and confirmed that my guerrilla gardening had been the best strategy for everyone.

If I was to prevent any further attacks I had to stop the council from resuming their 'gardening'. Their resumption of responsibility

GUERRILLA GARDENER AT PERRONET HOUSE SEEKS TRUCE.

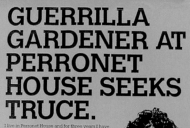

I live in Perronet House and for three years I have planted, weeded and cleared litter from the big flower beds around our home. From time to time I have had help too. This has all been free of charge but without permission. During these years Southwark Council have only gardened here once, (when they savagely pruned our big white Butterfly Bush just before it was about to flower). Yet until recently they were charging leaseholders (and presumably tenants too) over £40 each per year for "ground maintenance"!

This is scandalous. So far a refund for one year has been agreed but we deserve more. I want to continue gardening here as a volunteer but I now also want permission. They have agreed to give me permission if a majority of residents want me to continue. You will soon be asked in writing for your opinion. Please say YES!

For more information contact: richard@guerrillagardening.org or call 020 7261 1445.

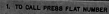

Let's fight the filth
with forks and flowers.

**GUERRILLA
GARDENING
.ORG**

---

1. TO CALL PRESS FLAT NUMBER
2. WAIT FOR REPLY
3. ENTER WHEN TONE SOUNDS

31   32   33   34

was not the victory I had been looking for. I decided to present myself as the alternative, a volunteer who was happy to continue tending the beds without any cost to them. I fired off an e-mail explaining this to a couple of local councillors. A week later one of them replied, agreeing to meet me by the beds. He took up my case, but the unelected officials who were ultimately responsible were confused about how to respond.

In seeking legitimization for gardening at Perronet House I put up posters making the case to residents that I should be allowed to continue.

Eventually, after more weeks of inconclusive telephone calls, a meeting was convened between myself and two officials from the estate office, their chief gardening contractor, a labourer and a horticultural expert from the other side of south London. They wore dark sunglasses and tired expressions.

The meeting immediately went off course. The horticultural expert pointed out issues he had with my planting, describing the one tomato plant (*Solanum lycopersicum*) as 'totally inappropriate for a flowerbed', warning me with a shaking head that the lilac (*Syringa vulgaris* 'Prince Wolkonsky') was invasive and predicting the laurels (*Laurus nobilis*) would get very big if I did not look after them – oblivious to the fact that (unlike his department) I would indeed be looking after them. The labourer insisted that the butterfly bush was a damaging weed and posed a threat to walls and railway bridges, but was blind to its safe location and unable to explain why, if it was so dangerous, he had merely cut it back rather than digging it out.

I lost patience with their nitpicking, the absence of an explanation for their neglect and their lack of appreciation for my voluntary contribution. I told them so, at which point the particularly twitchy senior contractor declared, 'Hey, this guy is completely unreasonable. Let's just chop the lot down.' This petty outburst provoked some sense from his colleagues and we moved on to discuss responsibility.

They were prepared to let me continue gardening on the understanding that I would give them at least one month's notice if

I wanted to stop. They seemed reassured that my intentions were benign and that my horticultural competence was strong, but they had their own issues to resolve. Crucially, the three contractors needed to explain to the council why, for years, they had not been doing the job of tending this area. Worse, it turned out that every tenant and leaseholder in the block had for years been paying a charge for the grounds maintenance of Perronet House, although no maintenance had been taking place. Some had got wind of the scandal and complained, and this had led to the council's resumption of 'gardening'.

However, many tenants were happy to have a refund instead and for me to continue gardening. Eventually the council told us they would cease charging for grounds maintenance and pay refunds for most of the period of neglect. They wrote to every resident in Perronet House declaring their support for me and inviting any complaints. Of course no one has complained, and now there is one location where I am no longer a guerrilla but a legitimate community gardener.

CONCESSIONS

Be prepared to concede something if you can see that the end result will be largely in your favour. At first just the thought of going legit may be an obstacle for you. The shift from radicalism to respectability raises the fear that your metaphorical well-worn army fatigues will have to be switched for something constrictingly neat and tidy. Battle, after all, is thrilling, whereas bureaucracy is boring, and working with the system feels to some like giving in to the system. This need not be the case. Do your best to stay away from red tape, and point out to the authorities that you have not wasted their time in the past and need not do so in the future. Set your tone right and you can offer the officials the energy and creativity they increasingly know they need to do their jobs better.

Some guerrilla gardens in New York had to be lost to enable the rest to be saved – a painful lance for the swollen boil that the pressure to allow them to be built on had become. Quite understandably, some community gardeners had great difficulty accepting this when the case was made in 2002. Adam 276 told me the story of these difficult times: 192 community gardens were still in limbo-land, poised for classification as part of the Department of Parks and Recreation, but frustratingly 'some far-left anarchist groups and men in flower suits refused to sit down at the table to discuss how best to do this'. Adam shook his head with the distressing memories of those days. 'Even a socialist utopia has rules,' Adam told the protesters, and he implored them to go legitimate so that the majority of gardens could be saved.

In Montreal, a group of community gardeners quite literally went up in the world when their garden had to be demolished to make way for a new building, because they were offered the new rooftop as a place for a fresh start. Elizabeth 650, who tends the Liz Christy Community Garden, is pragmatic: 'It is always going to be a dance between what is valuable to the community and the economic forces – there are still battles to be fought.' This attitude of give-and-take has recently helped the garden survive the pressures of a brand-new development springing up next to it.

When the time comes, you must be prepared to fight alongside conventional forces if they are willing. For us, this means professional employed gardeners. I leave them to do the lawn mowing; you may have other requests, such as waste removal or fence construction. Even the first guerrilla soldiers fighting Napoleon in the Peninsular War did not beat him single-handed: the conventional British army led by the Duke of Wellington hammered Napoleon's forces from the Portuguese side of Spain, driving them towards the resilient guerrilla fighters in the Pyrenees. These guerrillas sacrificed nothing to the British in return for the support.

ALWAYS A GUERRILLA

With your guerrilla days behind you it will be a love of gardening, not the illicit aspects of the activity, that keep you actively involved. Some people miss the mischief, but remember that your legitimate garden began as a guerrilla garden. No one can take that away. Your strategy worked: your garden is living proof.

I asked Samantha, my estate manager at Southwark council, whether she would have given me permission to garden had I asked at the outset, and she replied without a moment's thought: 'Absolutely not.' This will always make the garden more special to me. Three years of just getting out there and doing it, and then putting the council in the win-win position of being able to offer residents a better service for less money, was what made it possible.

While you may be more respectable now, you are also a dormant guerrilla gardener, a sleeper cell waiting for a reason to resume active service. If the rules you accepted stop making sense, challenge them. We have seen how the community gardeners in New York reverted to guerrilla tactics to protect their gardens from development. In Devon, Margaret 2878 assumed a combative mode to good effect when her council reneged on their agreement to clear her green waste. She threatened to withdraw the Torre churchyard from her town's entry for the prestigious Britain in Bloom competition, knowing that it was the jewel in the civic crown. This threat rapidly led to the council resuming the agreement.

8.3 Inspiration

Your legitimization can have a greater impact on the landowner than you imagine. You may actually change the way they think about their land. I know of three cities where the authorities have been directly inspired by guerrilla gardening on their turf.

NEW YORK CITY, USA

In response to guerrilla gardening, in 1978 the New York City authorities started a support organization called Green Thumb. They provided training and materials for those who wanted to create community gardens, and they significantly reduced the need for guerrilla activity by making it easier to garden legitimately. Green Thumb still exists today, helping over 600 volunteer-run gardens – which amount to an area as big as Central Park.

Admittedly most community gardeners I met in New York were fairly dismissive or unaware of Green Thumb's contribution, though this may be something to do with their leader's deliberately hands-off approach. Edie Stone, the director, thinks hard about her organization, and is keen to preserve the grassroots sense of self-sufficiency in the gardens. 'For example, we could give everyone identical sheds for their tools,' she says, 'but it's far better if they continue to make their own, using scrap wood in some, building grand double-decker pavilions in others.' The individuality and sense of achievement is therefore preserved. 'My challenge is to keep the bureaucracy at bay and let the gardeners do their own thing, to keep the guerrilla thing alive. Let them think in their own way. Let creative things happen.' She admits the battle spirit is important: 'Yes, I do want people to struggle!'

Guerrilla gardening has been important in revitalizing New York. Adam 276 showed me parks around Hells Kitchen that the city has recently renovated. 'We raised the bar,' he said, 'and the Parks Department had to follow.'

The New York City Parks Department has, in fact, taken up guerrilla gardening recently. They have introduced a new law that authorizes the planting of trees on private land if the owner cannot be found. At what point the search for the owner stops and gardening begins is vague, but my impression is that the enquiries do not last long and the gardening begins swiftly. 'It became quite clear that if

we had to wait for a landlord or owner's approval we would be waiting for ever,' said Bram 2112, deputy director of forestry for the Parks Department: 'If people don't want a tree we're going to have to deal with that later.' He and Gillian 2111 of TreesNotTrash.org have battled against the obsolete industrial landscape of Bushwick by planting more than 60 trees in front of abandoned warehouses and desolate lots.

Guerrilla activity has matured into this elaborate garden behind the terraced homes of Johannapark, Amsterdam.

AMSTERDAM, THE NETHERLANDS

This is a city more famous for watery streets than green streets, but the shortage of dry land has been one of the reasons why its citizens have learnt to make the most of it.

Guerrilla gardening began here in the early 1980s, in the inner city area called De Pijp. Nowadays this is a popular gentrified neighbourhood, but back then it was an area of abandoned properties in which a thriving community of ingenious squatters made use of the space. Although riots and clashes with police were common in Amsterdam at this time, so were less confrontational acts of protest. Some squatters decided to make themselves gardens in the street by removing the paving slabs that butted up against the façade of their occupied buildings. In this small gap, sheltered beneath a wall, plants could grow and decorate the edge of the pavement. The authorities were at first oblivious, then tolerant, and by the 1990s were finally inspired to change their official policy and encourage what had begun as guerrilla gardening.

The city now offers to remove the slabs if the neighbouring residents want a garden. On one day each May the district authorities create more of these *geveltuinen* (façade gardens), and in a party-like atmosphere paving stones are torn up, soil is dumped for the new beds and plants are handed out. Rules are minimal: the space must protrude no more than 30cm from the wall, and plants with thorns are banned. I met Saskia Albrecht, a garden designer who is employed by the city to give façade gardeners training. She encourages simple designs, blocks of colour, big foliage against a bold wall. The city is dotted with a great variety of these slit-shaped patches. While busy lizzies (*Impatiens walleriana*) burst from one, next door a sweet-smelling chocolate vine (*Akebia quinata*) is climbing.

Margreeta 898 pushed the rules a little bit further by filling both her official façade garden and tubs along the curb on Brederodestraat. When the authorities removed them, she complained and they relented, demonstrating once again that in this city guerrillas tend to win.

VANCOUVER, CANADA

On their website the city of Vancouver reminds people why they once discouraged people from planting in public: the guerrilla gardener faces electrocution (from buried cables, that is, not as punishment) and a pedestrian risks stumbling over wayward plants. However, they changed their minds.

The turning-point came after an accidental act of guerrilla gardening in 1994. It occurred in Mount Pleasant, where a network of new roundabouts and corner bulges had just been built. A load of compost had been dumped by the construction workers at the corner of Manitoba and 14th in preparation for planting later in the year. But while the soil was still bare a local resident intervened by cleaning his bird feeder out on to the ground. The birdseed unexpectedly sprouted into dozens of sunflowers, a spectacular traffic-calming display that looked quite unlike the usual civic planting.

Vancouver City Hall started getting phone calls from people asking if they could plant the traffic circles and corner bulges near their homes. Others wondered if they could take care of the plants the city provided. Enough interest was generated for the city to start a pilot project, and in 1994 the Green Streets Program was born, initially with fifteen volunteers. The city provides lots of guidance, helping to make their work as easy and uncontroversial as possible – for example, planting should be set back at least 30cm from the pavement to avoid obstructing pedestrians, a high-visibility jacket and gardening in daylight are encouraged, and soil and plants are sometimes made available.* A green sign marking a roadside indicates that the plot is available for someone to look after, and a yellow sign lets passers-by know that someone is caring for it.

Hundreds of volunteer gardeners now tend over 250 Green Streets gardens across the city. Vancouver recognizes the value: the Green Streets page on the city's website proudly proclaims that it 'encourages and promotes a sense of community pride and ownership which ultimately benefits the entire city'.

8.4 Compromise

Your guerrilla garden is safe, the authorities are on side, but your celebrations may still be tempered. In your victory there may be a few losers, and you may need to accept that a win-win situation is not entirely possible.

Disturbing a neglected landscape can displace wildlife. It is not just animals that may become homeless: consider also the vagrants, drug dealers and street workers who felt comfortable among the dereliction. Transforming a neglected area piecemeal will give time for wildlife to move on slowly, without confrontation, and if you work sensitively you may be able to accommodate and attract less antisocial wildlife – but you must accept that you will make some creatures homeless. (If moving on antisocial street life is actually part of your intention, there may still be a compromise, in that the problem could just have been displaced elsewhere.)

* Vancouver's Green Streets advice is useful for any guerrilla gardener. Read it at http://city.vancouver.bc.ca/engsvcs/streets/greenstreets/guidelines.htm.

Fencing a guerrilla garden is controversial because it appears to separate 'winners' from 'losers'. For those like me who tend tree pits, roadside verges and traffic islands this is not an issue; but for those battling to build safe recreational spaces for community gardens, it is a real dilemma.

A secure barrier safeguards plants and garden paraphernalia and deters fly tippers. Erecting hurricane fences was one of the first steps for New York guerrilla gardeners, and to this day most of the community gardens are enclosed by fences they are very proud of – the day I visited Zeedee 1635 at the Sixth Street and Avenue B garden volunteers were happily painting theirs. Access is granted via a variety of cash-for-keys distribution schemes or timetabled openings. Without the fences, New York's green oases would have faced a difficult future; but it is hard to escape the sad fact that land has been annexed where once it was accessible to anyone (albeit as a miserable mess). While fences aid the struggle against neglect, they do not help the other struggle, that against scarcity of land.

Peter 509, a guerrilla gardener in New York, is aware of the problem: 'We are helping to define what is public space. It is only public if it is open. You can appreciate it and stand next to it, but not really enjoy it and do yoga on the deck if it is not open. Some community gardens seem more like privatized spaces – it could be a restaurant you are going past – so people walk past and don't come in. People just assume everything is private now.'

This is a pity. Adam 276, a key-carrier to the Clinton Community Garden in New York, is well aware of this drawback too, and emphasized to me how they do their best to overcome it by ensuring that access and enjoyment of the garden are spread as far and wide as possible, with 6,000 key carriers, a garden designed with something for everyone, a wide range of activities and events as well as welcoming signage in three languages. The Clinton Community Garden is undoubtedly a guerrilla victory garden.

Some guerrilla gardeners do without fences altogether.* Daniel 1224 has a garden in the La Boca district of Buenos Aires, a rough area at night, but he 'locks' it with a gate secured by a thread. This symbolic suggestion of ownership has been sufficient to prevent any crime. The Rosa Rose Garden in Berlin has been open all hours for four years now, and although there has been a little vandalism, the gardeners see no need for fences yet. Both these gardens are in neighbourhoods where the community has solidarity with the garden.

But open access does not always work for guerrilla gardens. The guerrillas who built the People's Park in Berkeley, California, were keen to keep it open to anyone, particularly the fringes of society. In this they were victorious. But the cost of their openness was that the park developed a reputation as a hangout for drug users and criminals, thus excluding other members of the public. Even though there were no fences, a mental barrier was created and their achievement was diminished.†

8.5 Legacy

A great victory is one that lasts long after the battle is over. Consider how your garden can live on without you. Choose plants with a long life, a durable constitution or a propensity to rampant regeneration. Tony 830's Welsh poppies (*Meconopsis cambrica*), like Anne 1613's tulips and crocuses in Richmond, Virginia, will

* Some guerrilla gardeners make it their mission to remove fences. The Downtown De-Fence Project is a sister organization of the Toronto Guerilla Gardeners offering free fence-removal to willing homeowners, encouraging them to open up their front gardens to create a visually more sociable and trusting environment (publicspace.ca/defence.htm).
† Dan 110, who had called out the rallying cry 'Let's take back the park' back in May 1969, admitted in 2006 that the People's Park 'has now become a somewhat forlorn urban park ... It's a place that no longer reflects the will for independence of the campus community.'

(*Overleaf*)
The Clinton Community Garden in New York's Hells Kitchen was a heavenly setting for Independence Day celebrations in 2001.

look after themselves for a long time. Ron 235 has an enormous and long-term legacy in mind when he plants giant redwoods (*Sequoiadendron giganteum*) around England – all being well they can live for thousands of years. The legend of John Chapman and his apple tree-planting in Ohio lives on two centuries after he began – so much so that he is credited with planting nearly every apple orchard in the Midwest.*

Sow seeds in the minds of others. Do not let what you have learnt rot away when you move on, but instead pile it on to the collective mental compost heap, a rich resource for fertilizing new gardens. Your guerrilla gardening experiences and achievements can be inspiration. 'Guerrilla gardens are little universities,' says Aresh 1451. He sees them as banks of knowledge about how to grow food in dense urban settings – a skill that he believes must become more commonplace. 'To me we should take the guerrilla out there and make it everyday, wherever land is being wasted. You can call it guerrilla gardening, or Everyday Gardening, or Let's Heal the Earth Gardening.'

Do not expect your legacy to be a monument carved in stone.† Gardens are living things and should be allowed to evolve naturally. Edie Stone, director of Green Thumb in New York, is aware that for the gardens to thrive the social structure must also be alive. Openness to change and newcomers is critical. Let the form of a garden shift to accommodate this rather than forcing it to fossilize. Newcomers may have different ambitions from yours. In Quincy Street, Brooklyn, a community garden suffered because the elderly gardeners were

---

* This is according to *John Chapman – the Legendary Johnny Appleseed* by Karen Warrick (Enslow, 2001). In fact most apple trees do not live much beyond 100 years. However, some have been found that are nearly 200 years old, so it is possible that a few of John's original trees are still alive.
† Actually in 1963 John Chapman had a stone monument erected in his honour in a street named after him. The granite marker is located on Johnny Appleseed Lane in Leominster, Massachusetts.

adamant that it was only for them to read and relax in. The book lovers died with no one, literate or otherwise, to take over and the garden fell into miserable disrepair. Fortunately James 2315, a Quincy Street newcomer, saw the potential and began tentatively restoring it as a guerrilla gardener before his gesture quickly won support and legitimization.

I visited a second-generation guerrilla garden built in the corner of a yard at Berlin's Humbolt University that has taken on a fresh role. When Julia 013 moved on she left it to other students who have reinvented it from being a simple colourful corner into an elaborate encampment. I joined nineteen-year-old Sebastian 1583 and his friends Heiner 1582 and Benny 1584 for lunch in their newly constructed den, for which they used salvaged wood and sofas, and listened to how they are learning to look after the garden through trial and error.

I admit that there are some guerrilla gardens that I initiated in London without sufficient thought about how to ensure long-lasting victory. The patches were in Manor House and Stratford, well outside my usual south London territory, but too tempting to leave neglected. I found locals to help create elaborate gardens, and they assured me they would look after them, but the plots gradually slipped back into neglect. My long-distance rescue missions and attempts to involve local people became an impossible drain on resources and I gave up. The lesson is that victory will be more secure if battle is initiated by local people, who are more likely to have the personal drive and ambition to battle for as long as necessary. Away from home, fight alongside natural commanders, not rank-and-file troops. Your role should be that of an experienced but short-term ally. In Manor House and Stratford, I was regrettably a leader who abandoned his troops to fend for themselves.

Record what you do, take photos and keep a diary – there are many more tales to be written about guerrilla gardening. Old

Gerrard Winstanley (who as we have seen failed quickly as a guerrilla gardener) did at least leave his written legacy, which has inspired people ever since to take land for the benefit of the community. Lewis H. Berens summed this up in 1906 with eulogistic prose:

> *The seed he planted fell upon barren soil; but though so hardened by the withering frosts of ignorance, as to seem but as a dead stone, the vivifying sun of knowledge may yet stir its dormant potency, recalling it to life, to spring up and to develop into a stately tree, yielding its life-giving fruits, offering the welcome protection of its branches to all seeking rest and shelter beneath its shade.*

8.6 In Conclusion

(Overleaf, left. Clockwise from top) Adam 276, New York; Margot 623 and troops, London; the first Green Guerillas, New York; Johanna 2491, New York; the guerrilla gardening youth of Perronet House, London; Sam 2798 and troops, Chicago.

By breaking rules, guerrilla gardeners are challenging the conventions of society. Doing so in public space is a direct rejection of our political environment. As guerrilla gardeners most of us fight within a democratic society, a structure that is meant to be sufficiently free to hear opinions and accept them if the case is compelling. We are also mostly participants in a capitalist system, where everything has a price and resources are traded.

Most guerrilla gardeners evade the pigeonhole of political affiliation. Observers label us as being all over the political map – a mayor of New York has described guerrilla gardeners as communists,* the Adam Smith Institute (a right-wing think tank) has expressed support for GuerrillaGardening.org, while journalists describe us as anarchists and culture jammers. Guerrilla gardeners

---

* In January 1999 Rudolph Giuliani, speaking on his WABC radio show, defended his policy of replacing community gardens in New York with housing by saying, 'This is a free-market economy. The era of communism is over.'

themselves variously describe their approach as communist, egalitarian, situationist, libertarian, spiritual, therapeutic and even fascist; I describe it as common-sense.

Many thriving community gardens that began as guerrilla activity are now microcosms of a different kind of society, one that is happier, more sociable and sustainable. Even a transformed roadside verge signals the potential for change. We know we should take greater responsibility for the health of the planet by changing our patterns of consumption and production. Gardening is one step in the right direction – and guerrilla gardening is making that step regardless of the obstacles. Choosing to cultivate someone else's neglected land is taking responsibility where others have not.

But politics and sustainability aside, the reason I became a guerrilla gardener is because I love gardening. If I lean out of the window of my high-rise flat, I see below a thriving flowerbed in the street where once there was filth. I feel proud. It is a victorious landscape. But I am also reminded that the fight in a garden is never over – the butterfly bush (*Buddleia davidii*) is a scraggly mess and must be pruned tonight.

(*Overleaf, right.
Clockwise from top*)
Ground Hog 1698,
Amsterdam; Tree-0-5
guerrillas, Miami;
Andrea 3534 and
Milanese guerrillas;
Margaret 2878 and
churchyard guerrillas,
Torre, Devon;
Ced 144, Huby,
Yorkshire; Julia 013,
Berlin; Rosie 1485
and guerrillas,
Vauxhall, London.

INDEX

Page numbers in *italics* refer to illustrations.

Acknowledgements

Thanks to the following guerrilla gardeners for the time and tales they have shared with me: Saskia Albrecht, Joe Allen, Andrew Beauchamp, Ellen Belcher, Peter Bowser, Heath Bunting, David Burns, Buster, Freda Byrom, Bill Canaday, Sean Canavan, Skye Caswell, Jonathan Clark, Jerry Coleby-Williams, Aimee Corbett, Christine Cowin, Peter Cramer, Alex Crane, Elizabeth DeGaetano, Tom Deiters, Namita Devidayal, James Doran, Andy Ensor, Malcolm Everton, Margaret Forbes-Hamilton, Luc Forest, Steve Frillmann, Cedric Frost, Al Girling, Ella Good, Ground Hog, Severin Halder, Torgut Hanf, Daryl Hannah, Paul Harfleet, Ben, Lilly and Noor Hartshorn, Andrea Heavy Petal, Frauke Hehl, Adam Honigman, Katie Hughes, Lucy Hughes, Julian Hull, Chris Humes, Aresh Javadi, Esther Jury, Louise Keane, Mike Kraus, Jim Kulbacki, Ron Levy, Donald Loggins, Thomas McMullen, Mario of Tip Top Mode, Qaies Masoud, Silvano Maxia, Denise Meredith, Kathryn Miller, Stephen Minshull-Beech, Oren Mizrahi, Sam Moulton, Aggie Murch, Helen Nodding, Christiana Piga, Poster Child, Alex Poulson, Adam Purple, Blair Randall, Hayley Reynolds, Janet Reynolds, Christian Richter, Chris and Tony Rickards, Heather Ring, Hannah Riseley-White, Angela Rossi, David Rourke, Sandy Sampson, Brita von Schoenaich, Zachary Schulman, Helmut Smitts, Matt and Jennifer Sparkles, Stephanie Spiegel, Edie Stone, Ryan Su, Doc Suzy, Michelle Thomasson, Justin Tilson, Ava Torre-Beuno, Matia Viegener, Ella von der Haide, Rachel Watson, Johanna Williams, Micah Wolfe, Erin Wood, Anne Wrinn, Austin Young, Andrea Zabiello.

Thanks to those around the world who provided me with memorable hospitality on my research trips: Oliver Francis in Oxford, Marcel Van Woerkom in Amsterdam, Girasol in Brussels, Johannes Kleske in Karlsruhe, Alice Foxley in Zurich, Clara Royer in Paris, Bob and Felicity Alexander in Brampton, Luc Forest and

Norman and Winda Pang in Montreal and Cory Claussen, Sarah Cremin, Dave Neubert, Buku Sarkar, and Eric Minton in New York.

Thank you to everyone at Bloomsbury, especially Richard Atkinson, Erica Jarnes and Natalie Hunt who have nurtured, weeded and pruned this book with ceaseless care; and thanks to Colin Midson, Jude Drake, Jason Bennet, Kate Tindal-Robertson and Penny Edwards who have got it out into the world. Thank you also to Will Webb and Billie Jean for the book's glorious design and illustration.

Special mention to all those I have guerrilla gardened alongside in London, particularly Sarah Anderson, Tom Ashworth, Kate Clark, Katherine Cowan, Pam Daruwala, Rosie Dogget, Stephen Frost, Naomi Gay, Clara Goldsmith, Andrew Haining, Gary Mack, Tim Osborne, Lyla Patel, Charlotte Ryland, Anne Slater, Joe Taylor, Stuart Thomason and Olly Zanetti.

Special thanks to Julia Jahnke, who generously shared with me her own guerrilla gardening research and welcomed me to Berlin for a wonderful week of discovery and debate; Tim Sarson, for his scholarly insight; my grandmother Margot Vickers, whose battles in the garden inspired me to pick up the habit; my teachers Stephen Tanner and Julian Tenby, who encouraged my young gardening experiments; Lyla Patel, for being there at the front line and the home front; Meike Suggars, for sharing and tolerating a flat more frequently filled with mud than flowers; Joan, my neighbour, who has cheered me onwards; David Noakes, for championing the legitimacy of my gardening; Rob Pepper, for coming to America with his camera and camaraderie and meeting the guerrillas; Matthew Yee-king, for his IT wizardry that launched the fragile GuerrillaGardening.org community and Jade Saunders, for finding and funding him; Alison Cutts, for first broadcasting news of its existence; Lizzie '002' Ambler, the perennially enthusiastic green-fingered friend who was first to enlist; and above all Chiki Sarkar, without whose guidance and encouragement this book would never have been written.

FOR FURTHER READING

For further reading, inspiration and advice please visit GuerrillaGardening.org. You will find a blog of my guerrilla gardening, reports of digs around the world, a community message board and links to other guerrilla gardeners. A bibliography for this book is at GuerrillaGardening.org/Bibliography.html.

PICTURE CREDITS

Thanks to the following people for their kind permission to reproduce the photographs in this book: Romuald 'Erdeurien' Abel p.158; Advertising archives p.39; Bodleian Library p.96; Bridgeman art library p.21; Daniele Del Castillo p.249 (Milan); Jonathan Clark p.174; Corbis p.88–9; Peter Cramer/Le Petit Versailles p.31; Terry Foss /AFSC.org p.105; Dallas Francis p.242–3; Cedric Frost p.249 (Yorkshire); Getty Images p.102; Hans Hanfstengle p.42; Todd Hellskitchen p.15 (New York); Michael Honer p.142; Christopher Humes p.120; Gavin Kingcome p.12, p.26, p.58; Krisztián Kolesár p.51; Erica Landau p.249 (Miami); Donald Loggins p.108, p.249 (Green Guerillas); Michael Mahoney and Verena Dauerer/pingmag.jp p.15 (Tokyo), Sam Moulton p.248 (Chicago); Helen Nodding p.80; Christian Richter p.162; Rosa Rose p.15 (Berlin), p.45, p.137; Sebastião Salgado/nbpictures p.59; Brita von Schoenaich p.86; Helmut Smits p.149; Joel Sternfeld p.82; Ryan Sue p.15 (Singapore); Jonathan Warren p.153, p.190; Steven C. Wilson p.68, p.171; Dan Wooller/Wooller.com p.8. All other images © Richard Reynolds.

A NOTE ON THE TYPE

The body copy is set in Sabon, cut in 1967 by Jan Tschichold. It is loosely based on the sixteenth-century typeface Garamond. Sabon takes its name from Jacob Sabon, the French punchcutter whose widow married Konrad Berner. The title and chapter headings are set in Page No. 508, a die-cut wood type designed in 1887 by William H. Page for his firm Page & Setchell of Norwich, Connecticut, USA. Page led the American wood type industry and was a community activist and lover of ornamental gardening.

Published by Bloomsbury USA, 175 Fifth Avenue, New York, NY 10010.
Distributed to the trade by Macmillan.
Library of Congress Control Number: 2008922473
ISBN-13 978-1-59691-449-0
First U.S. edition 2008

Design by willwebb.co.uk
Illustrations by billiejean.co.uk

10 9 8 7 6 5 4 3 2 1

Printed in Great Britain by Butler and Tanner, Frome.

Mixed Sources
Product group from well-managed forests and other controlled sources
www.fsc.org Cert no. SGS-COC-1722
© 1996 Forest Stewardship Council